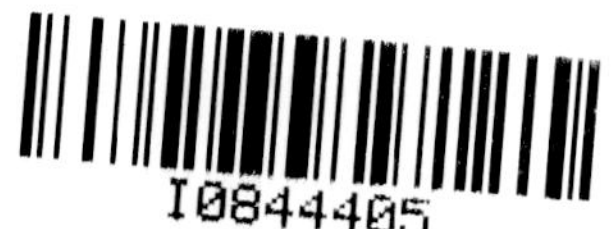

I0844405

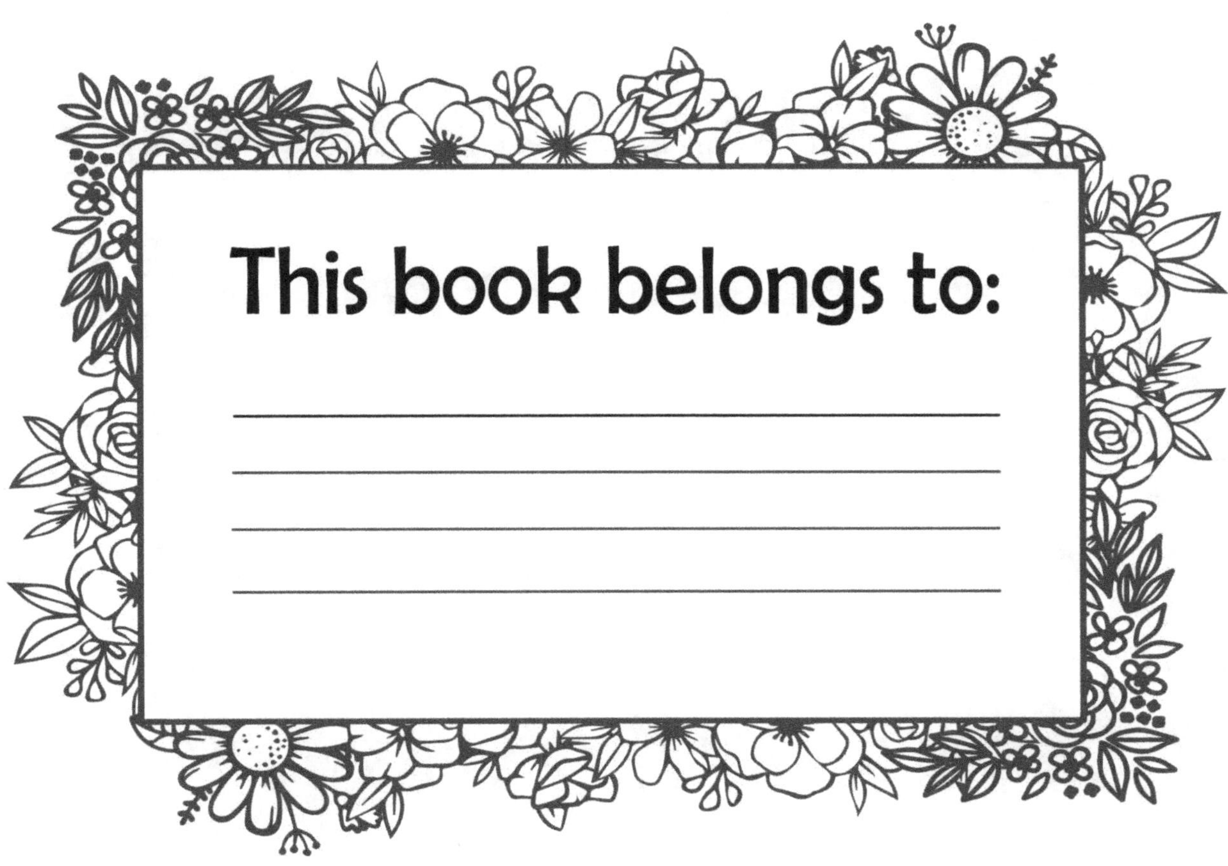

This book belongs to:

COLOR TEST PAGE

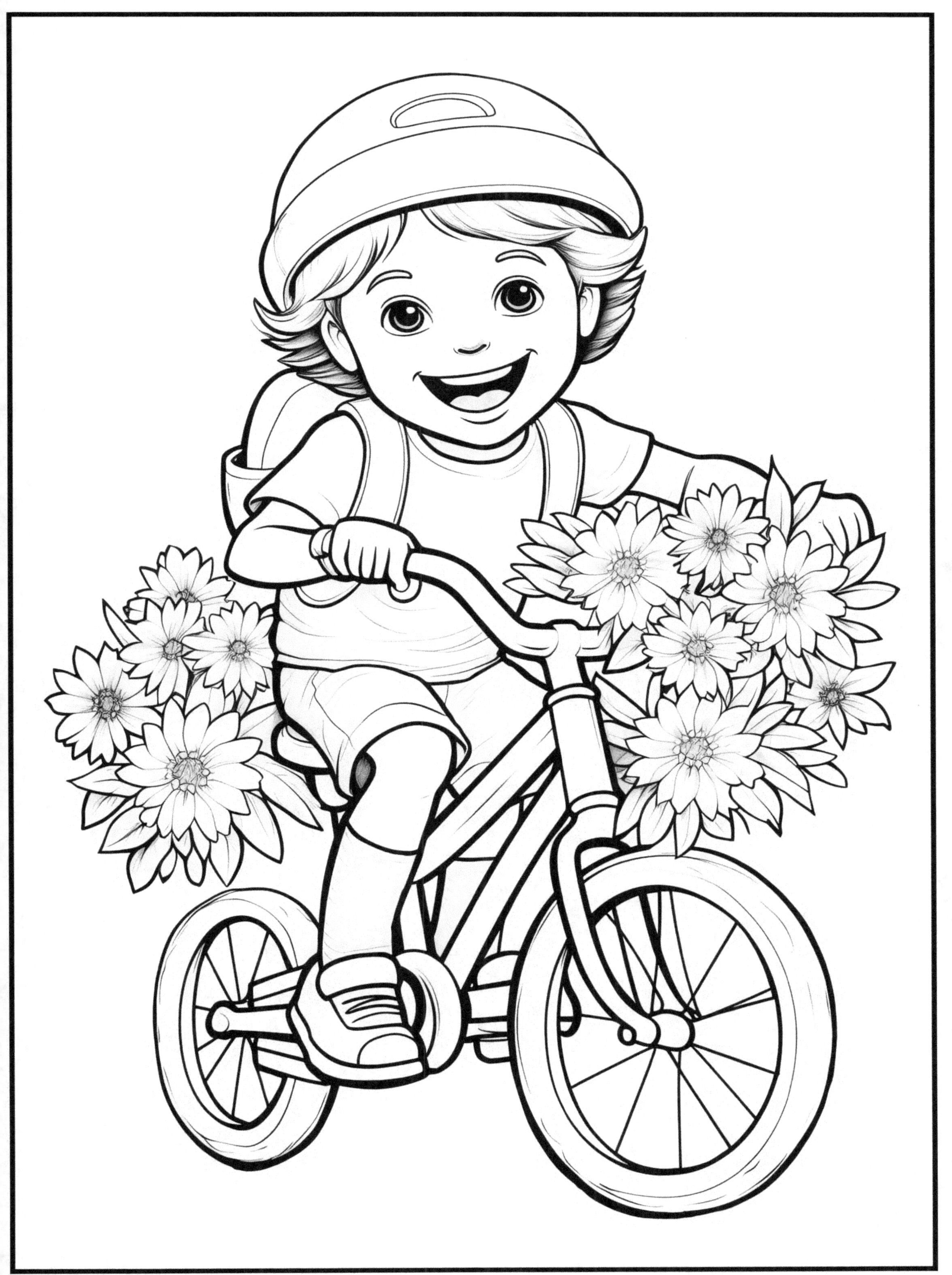

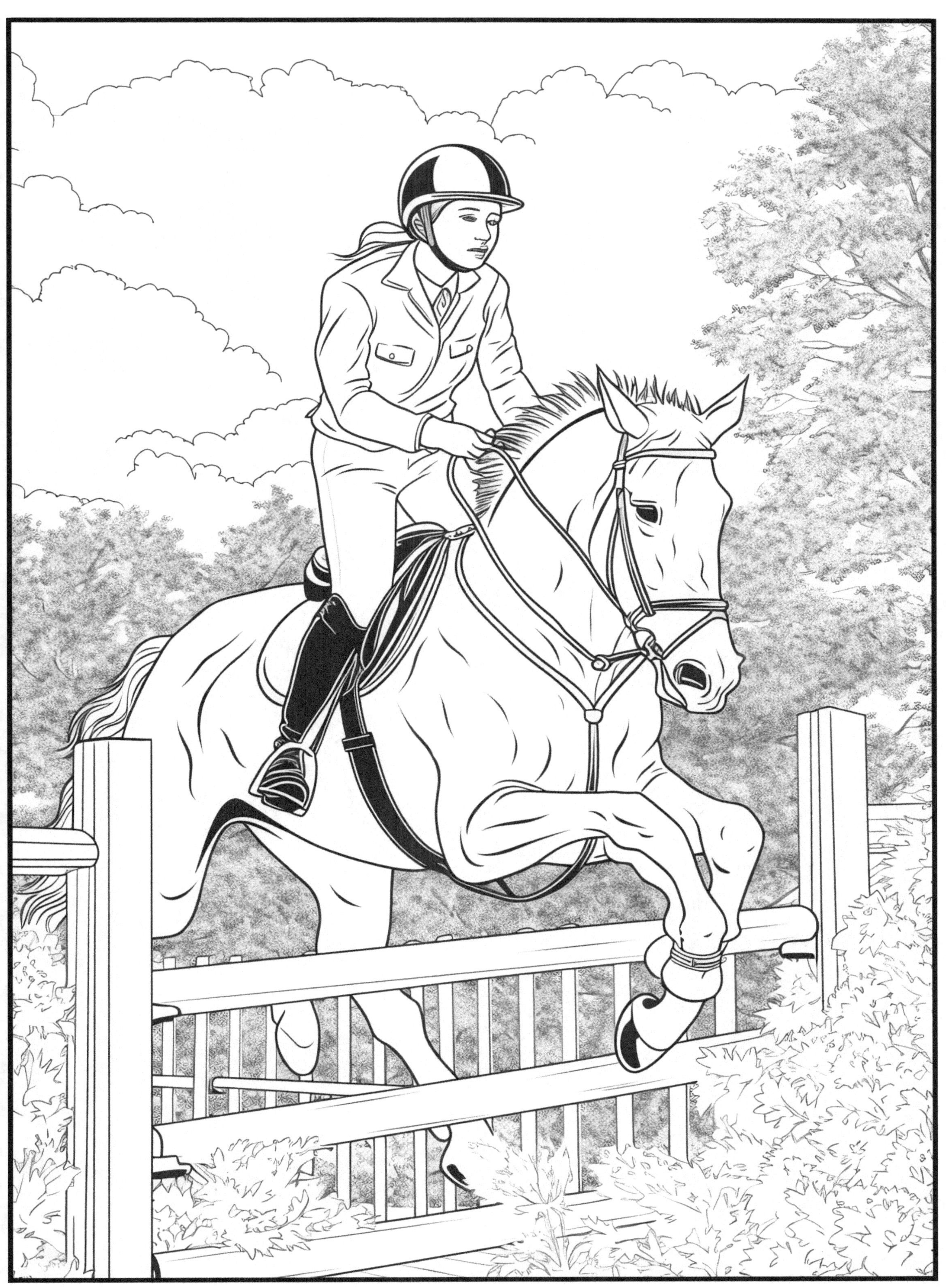

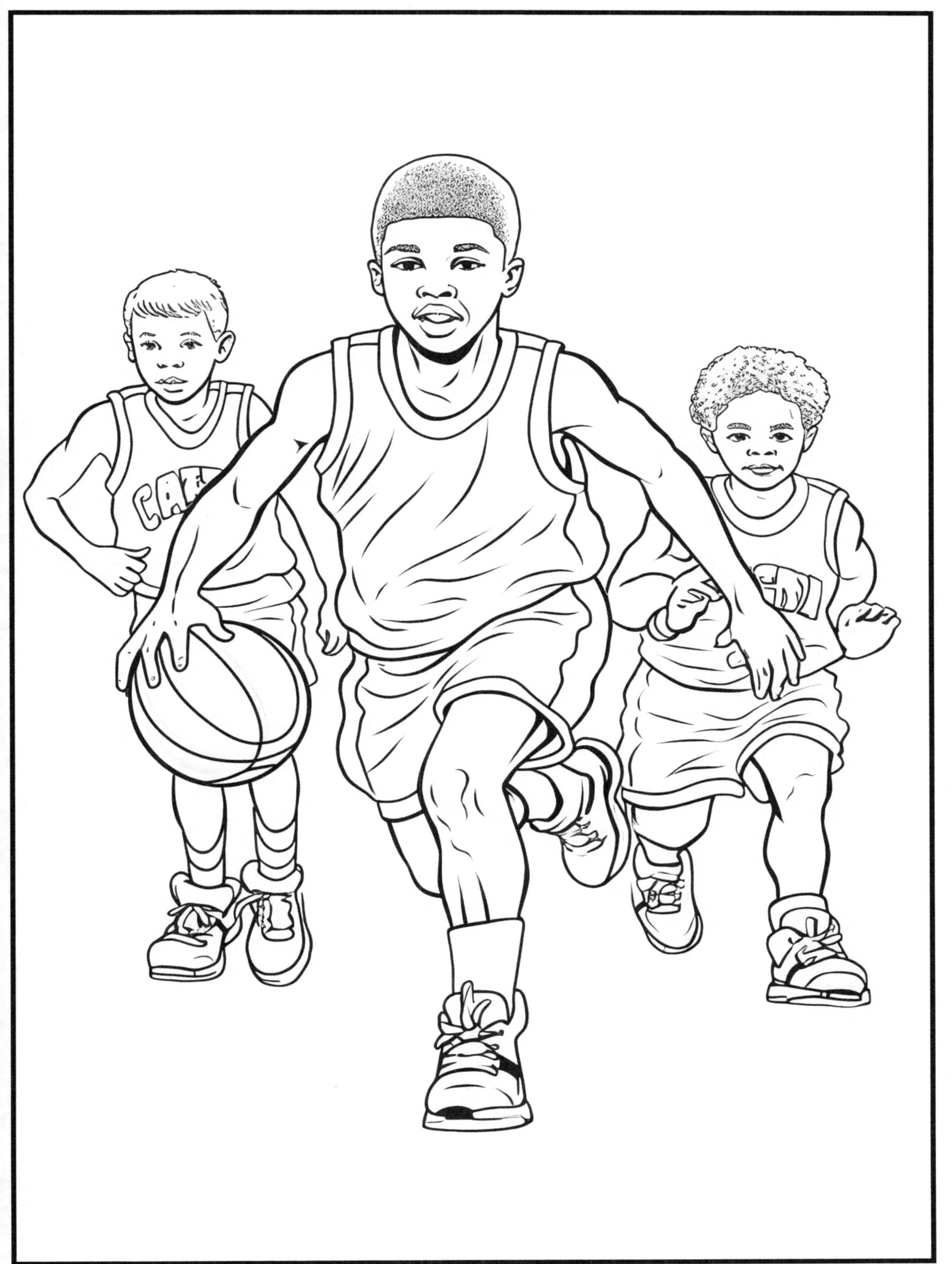

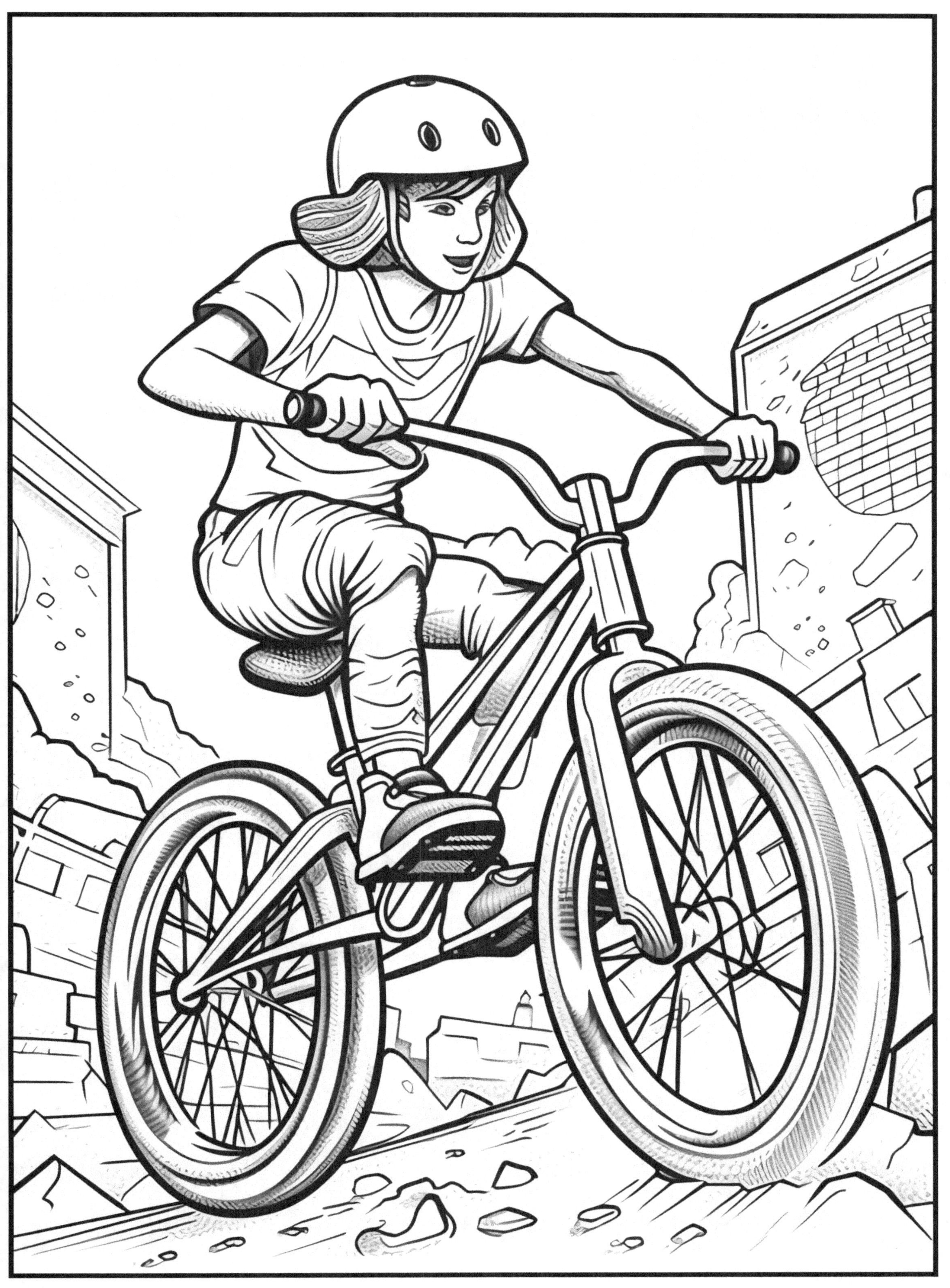

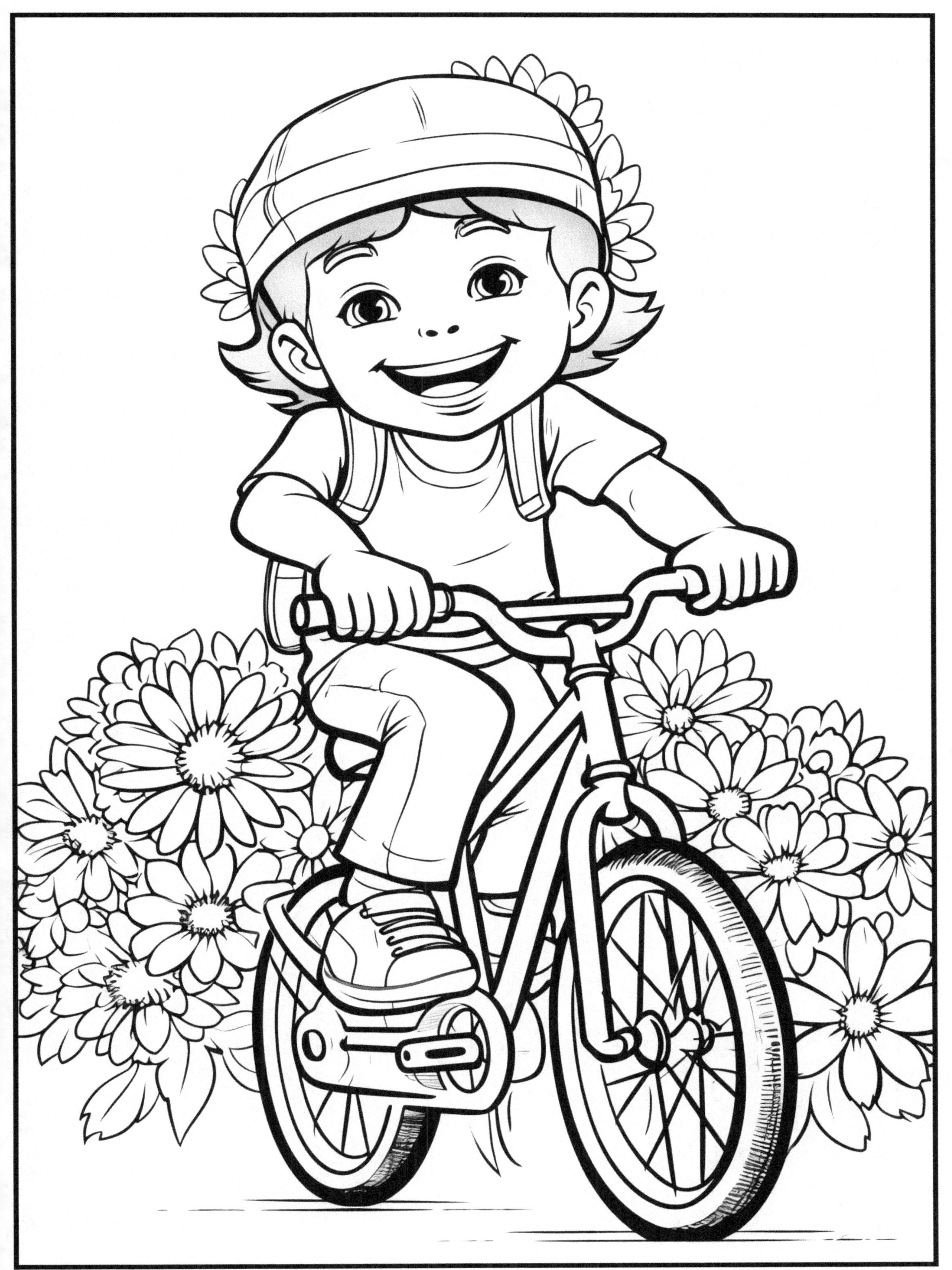

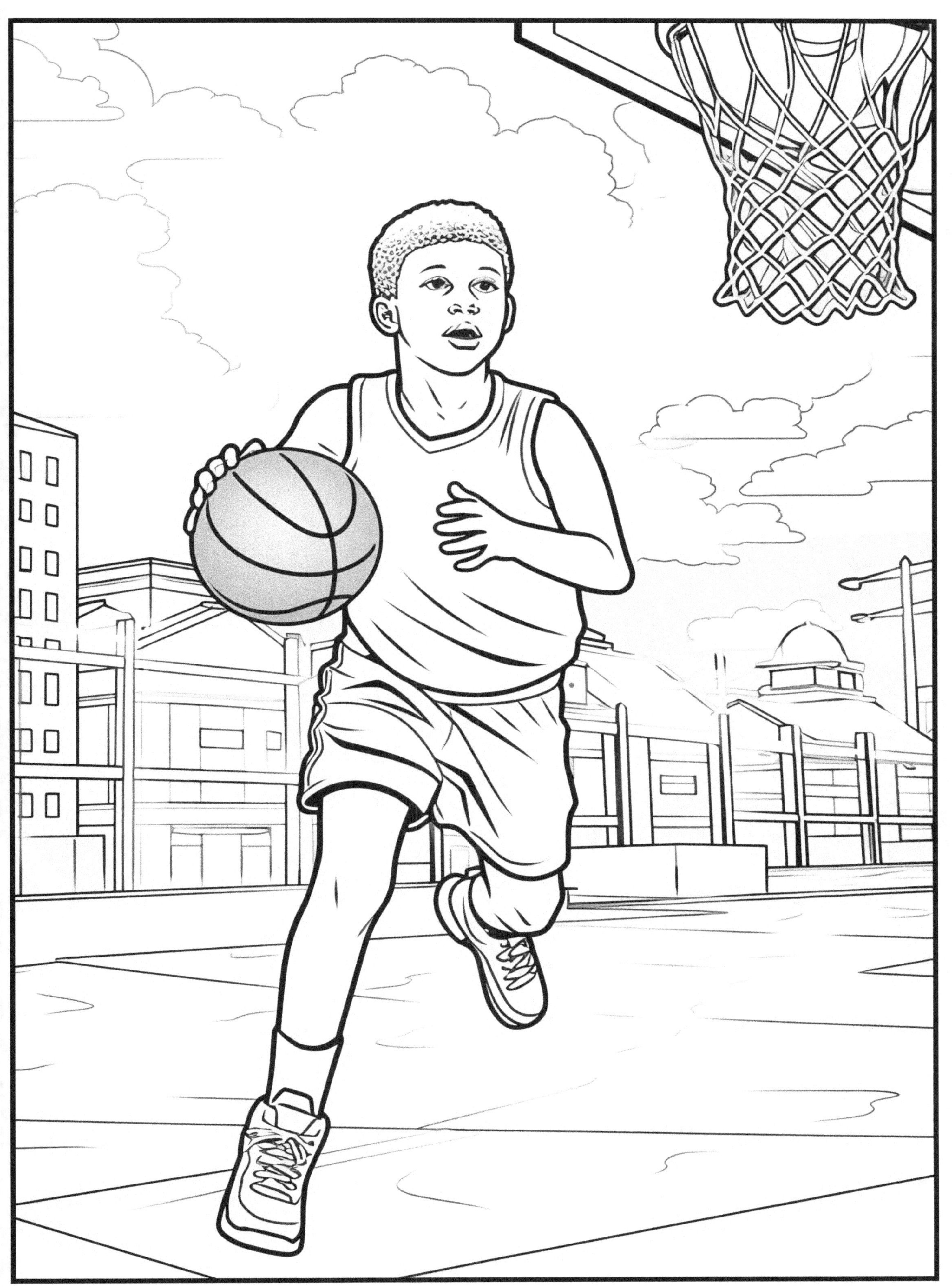

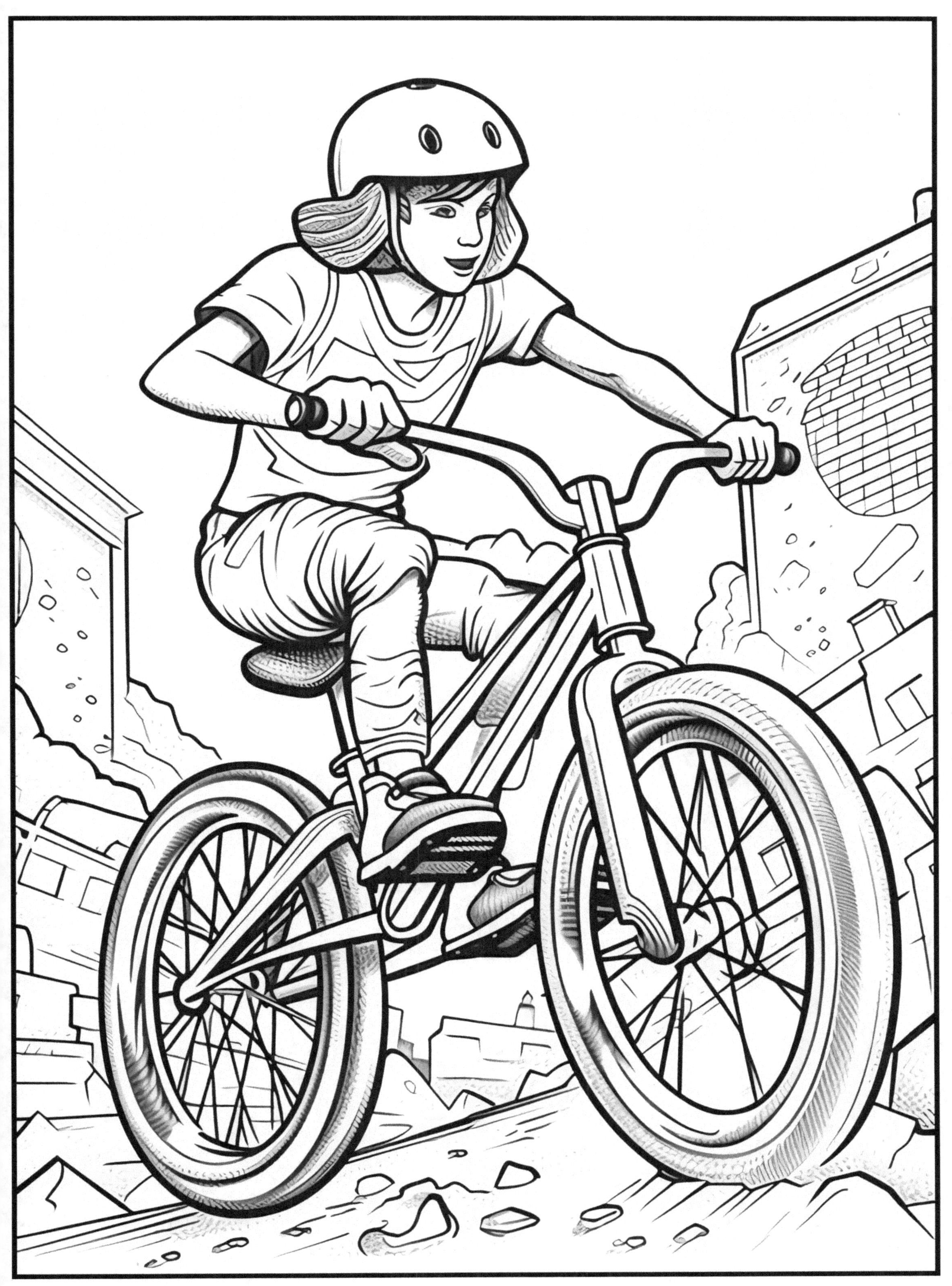

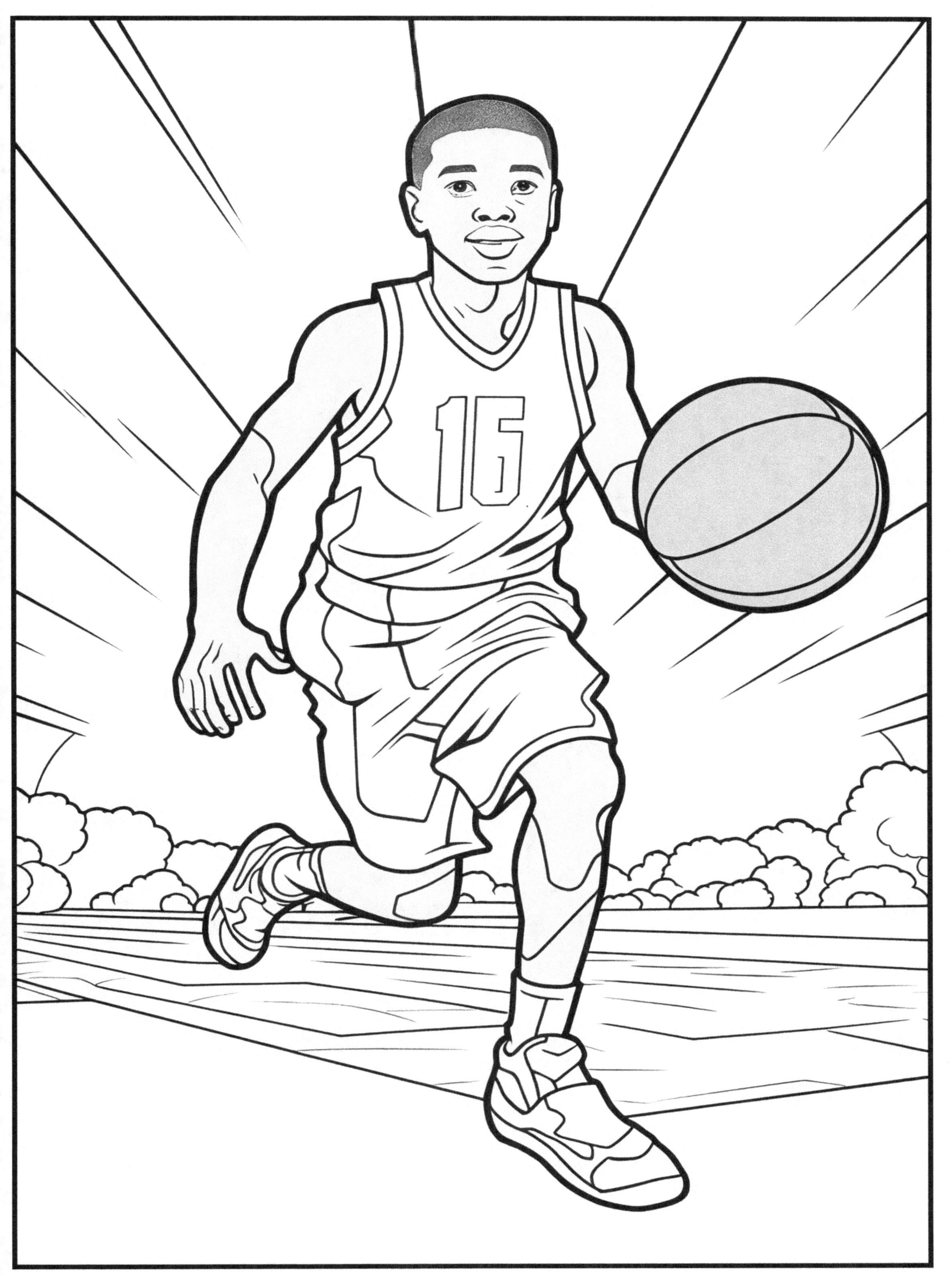
16

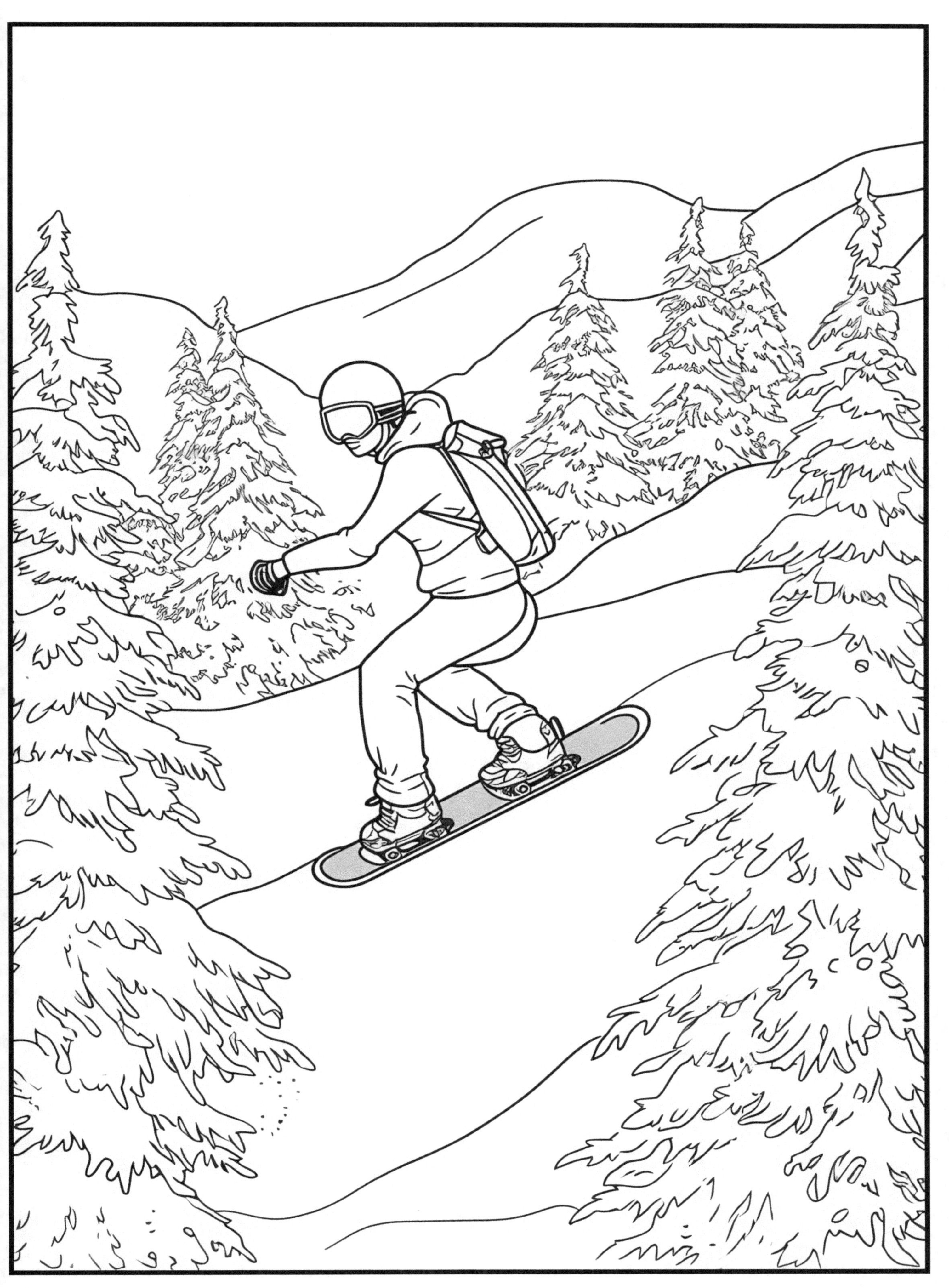

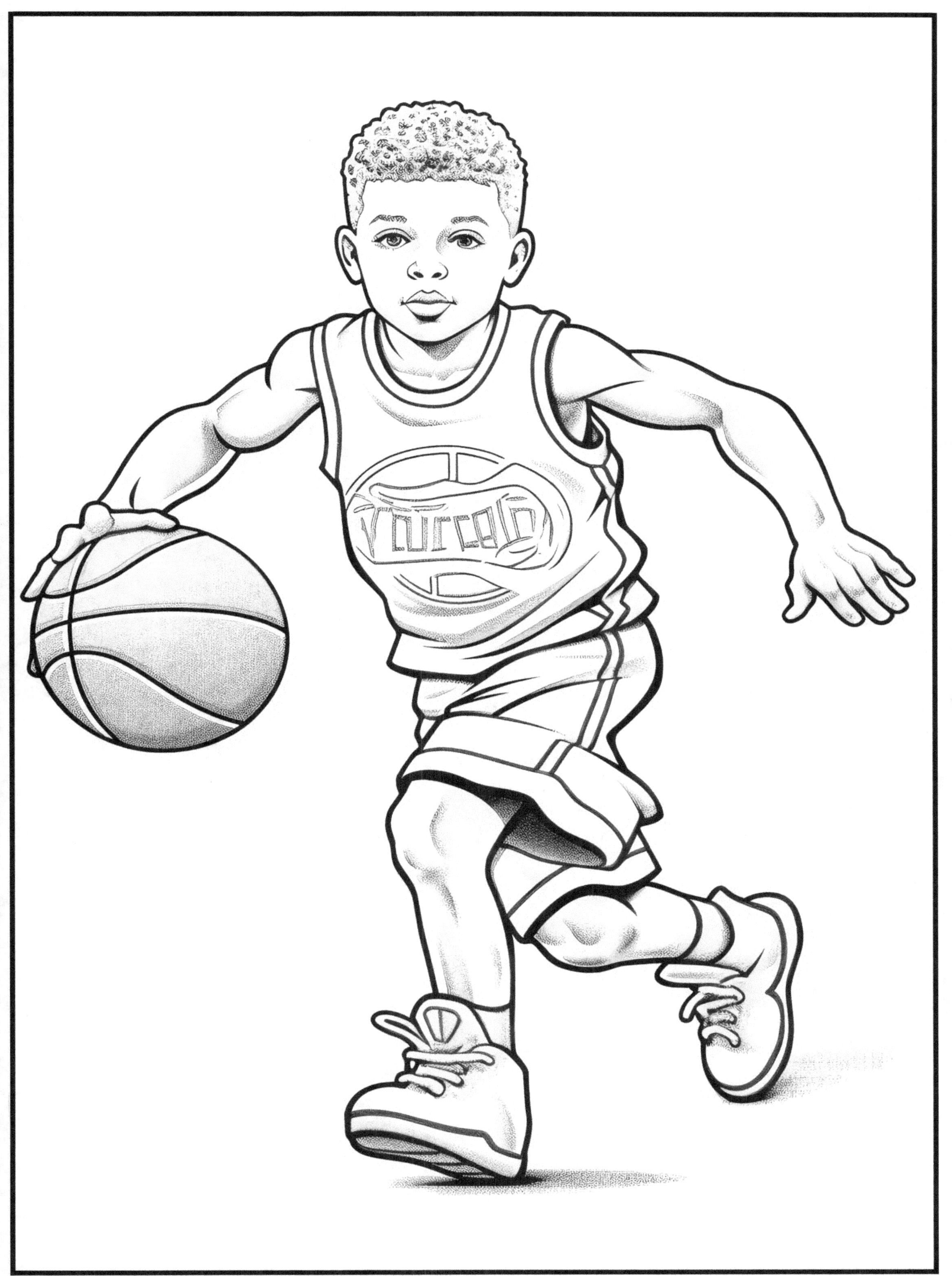

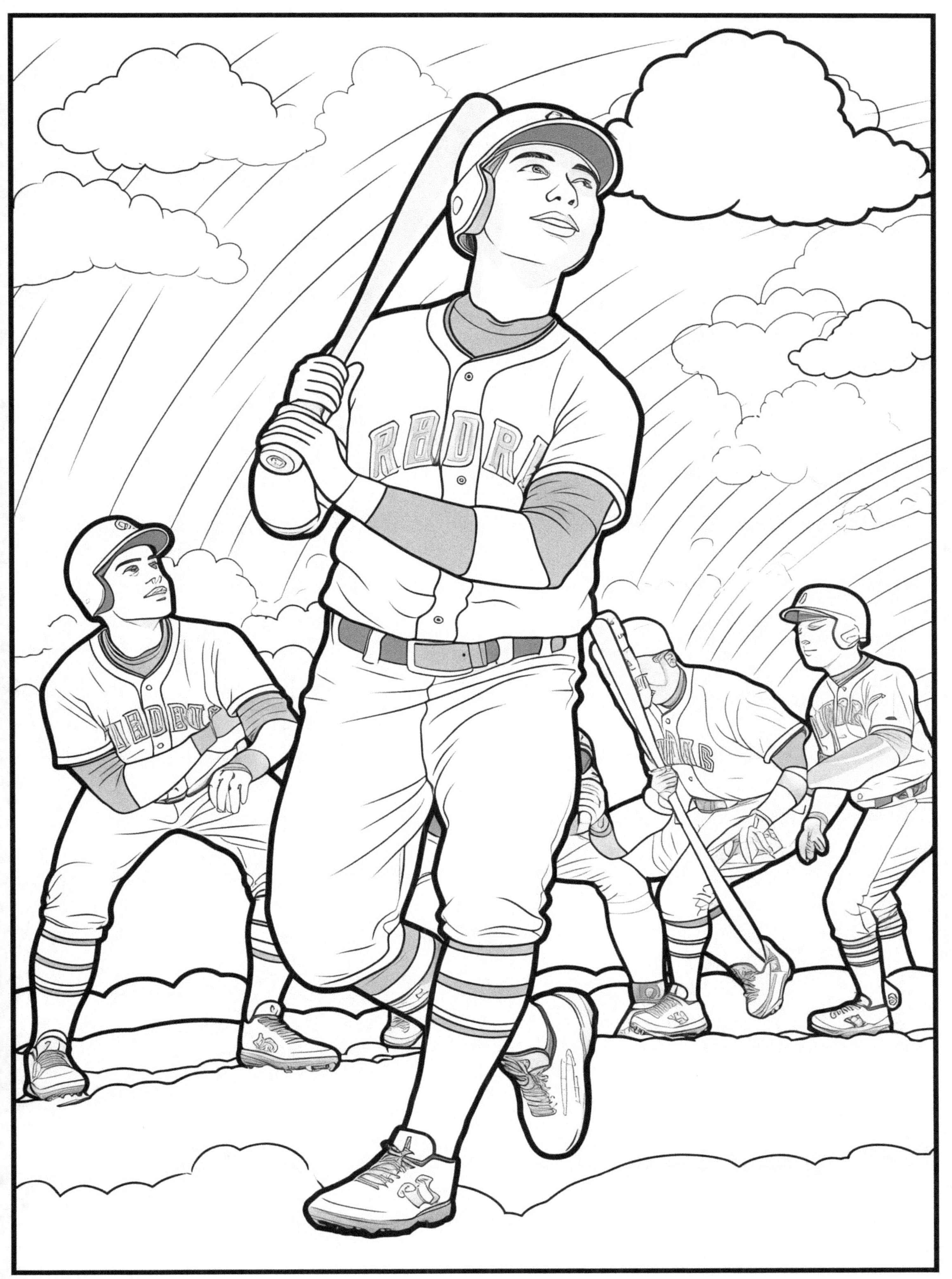

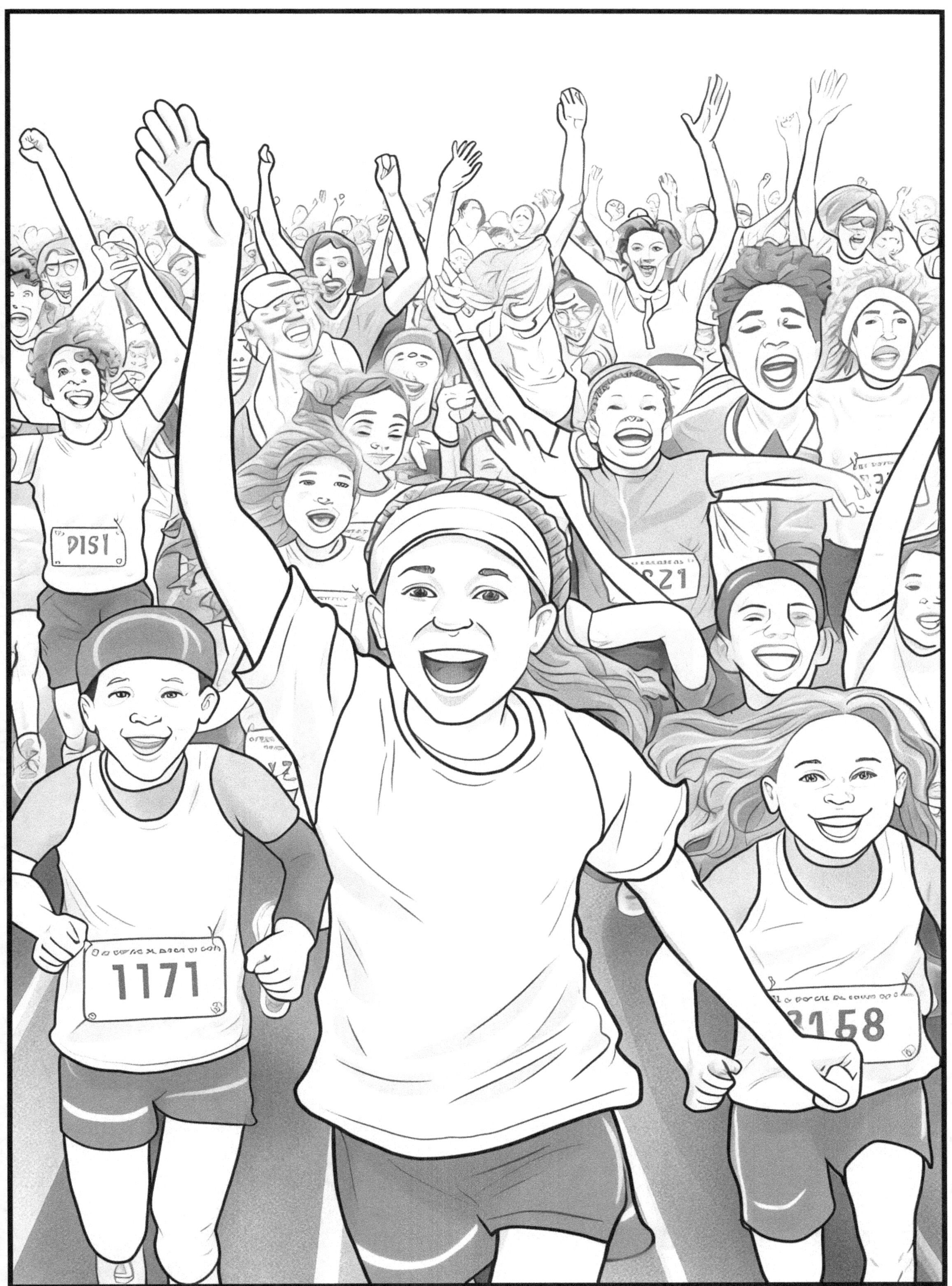

P151
1171
3158

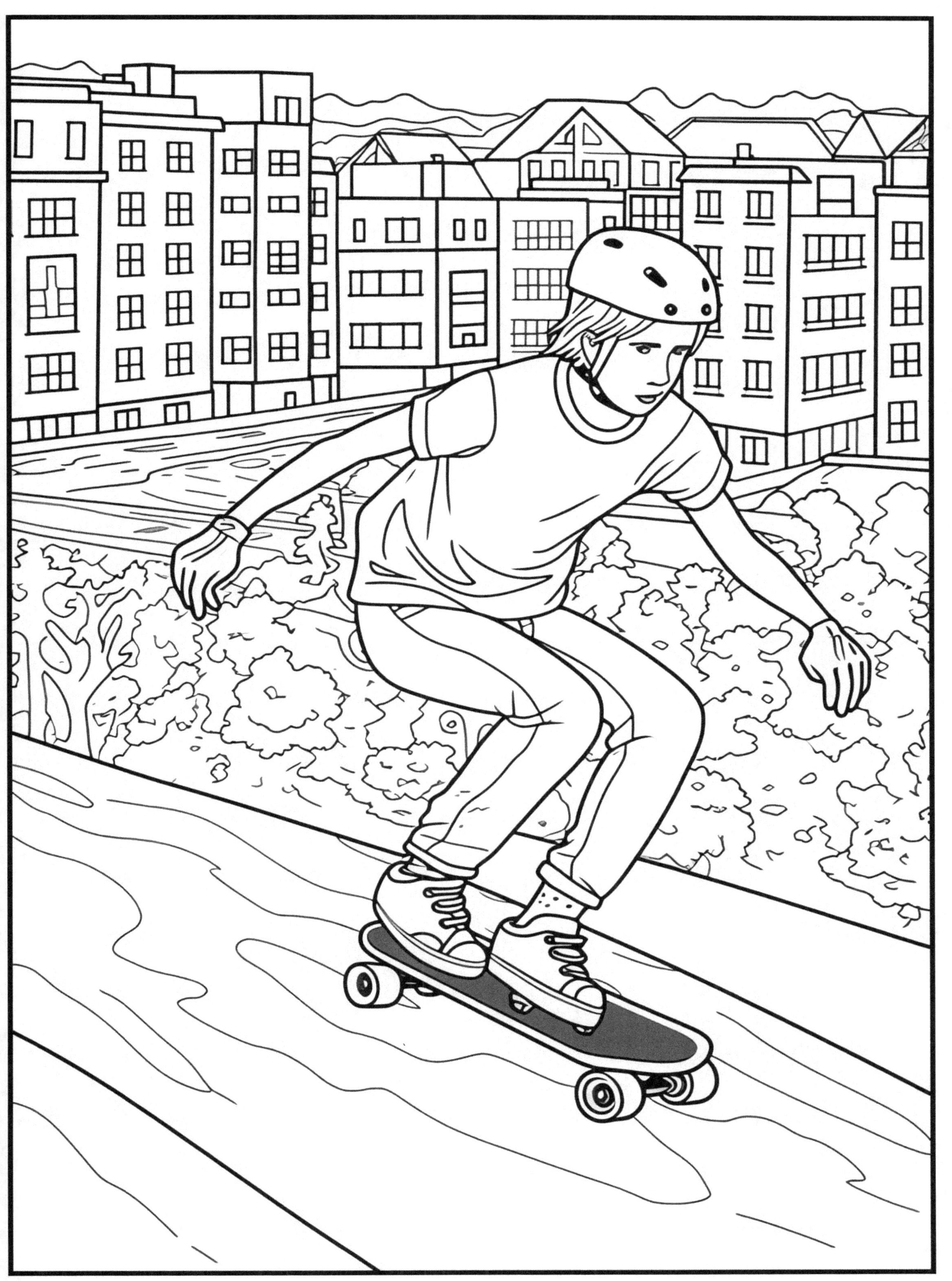

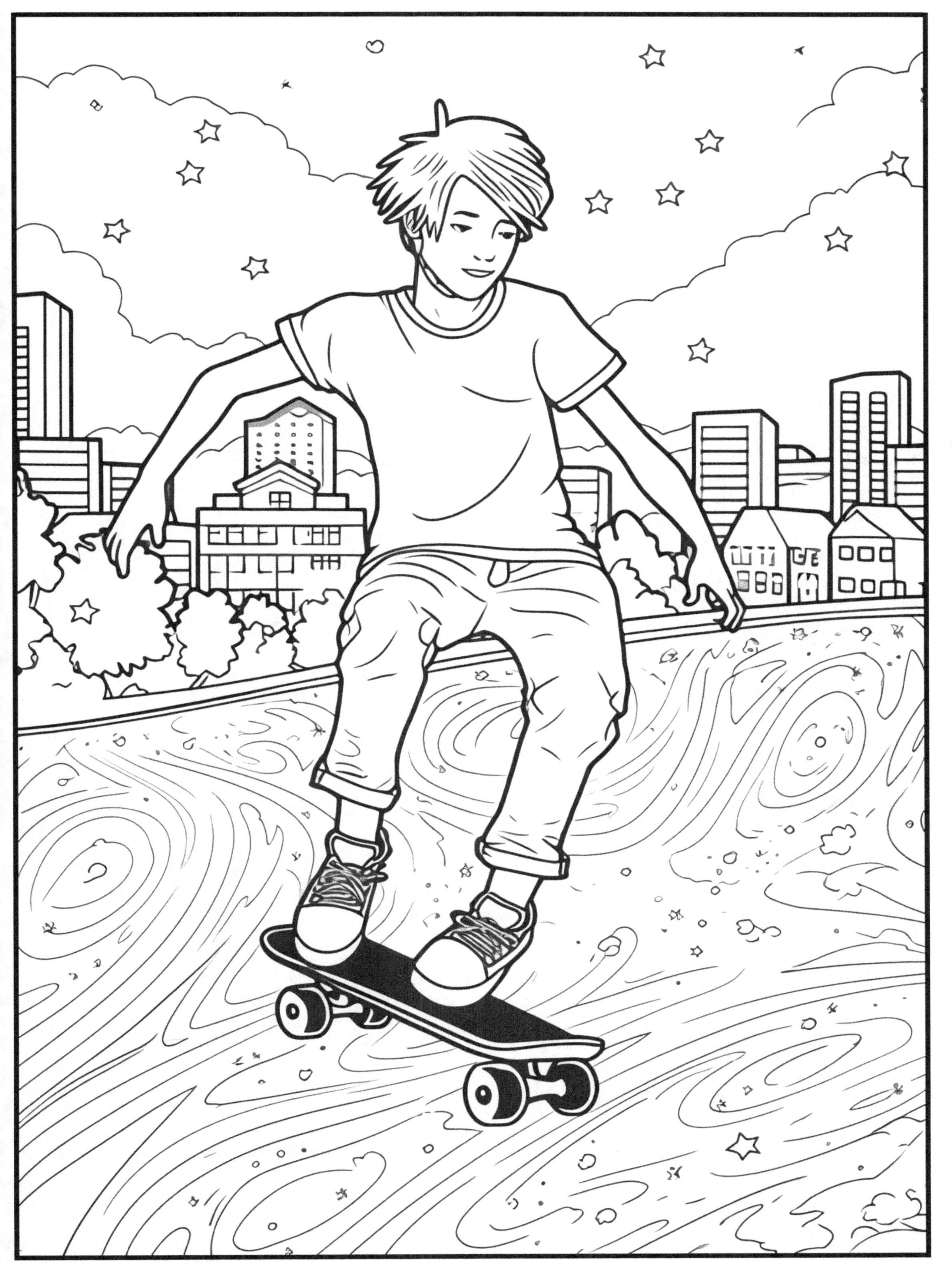

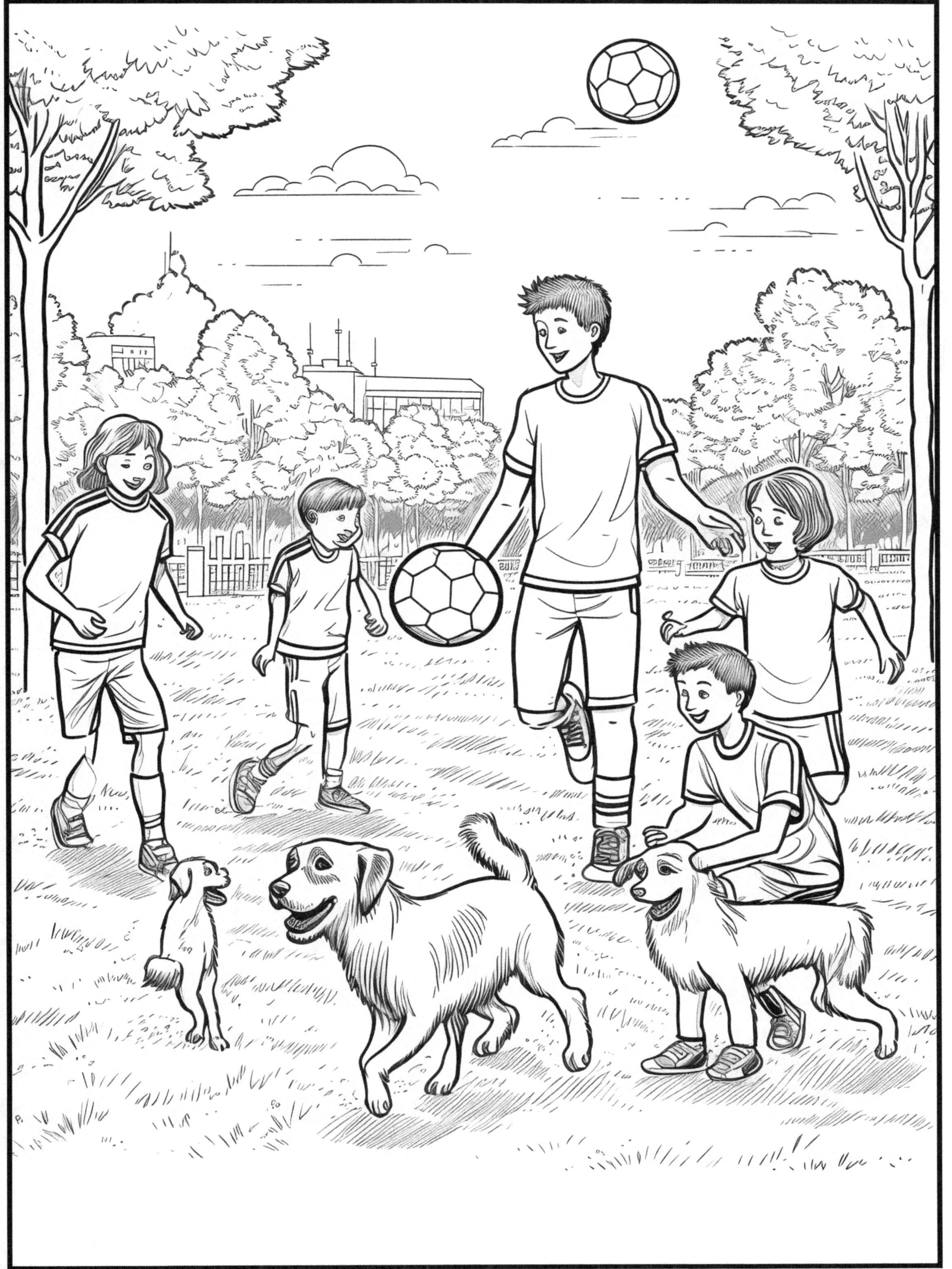

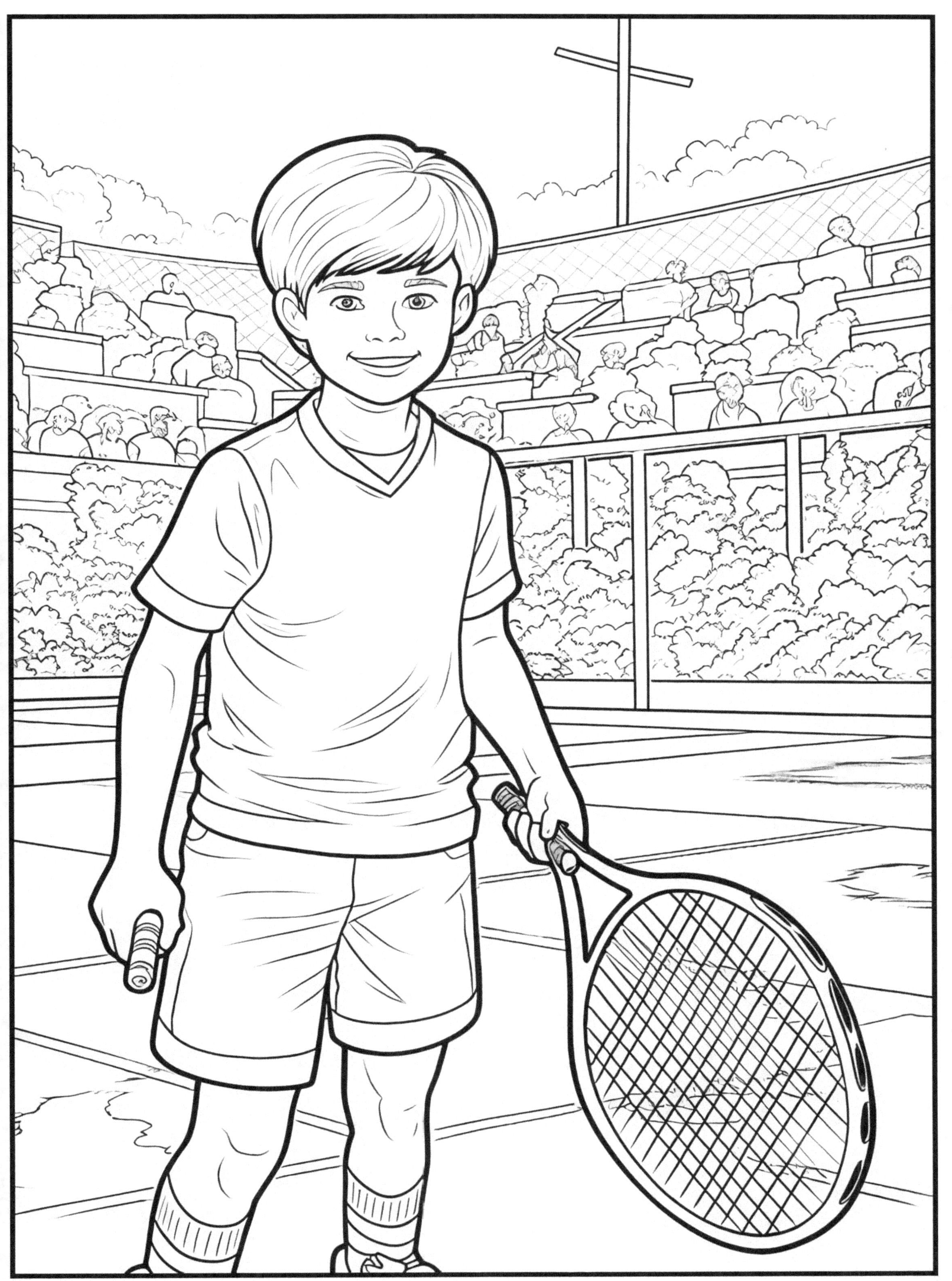

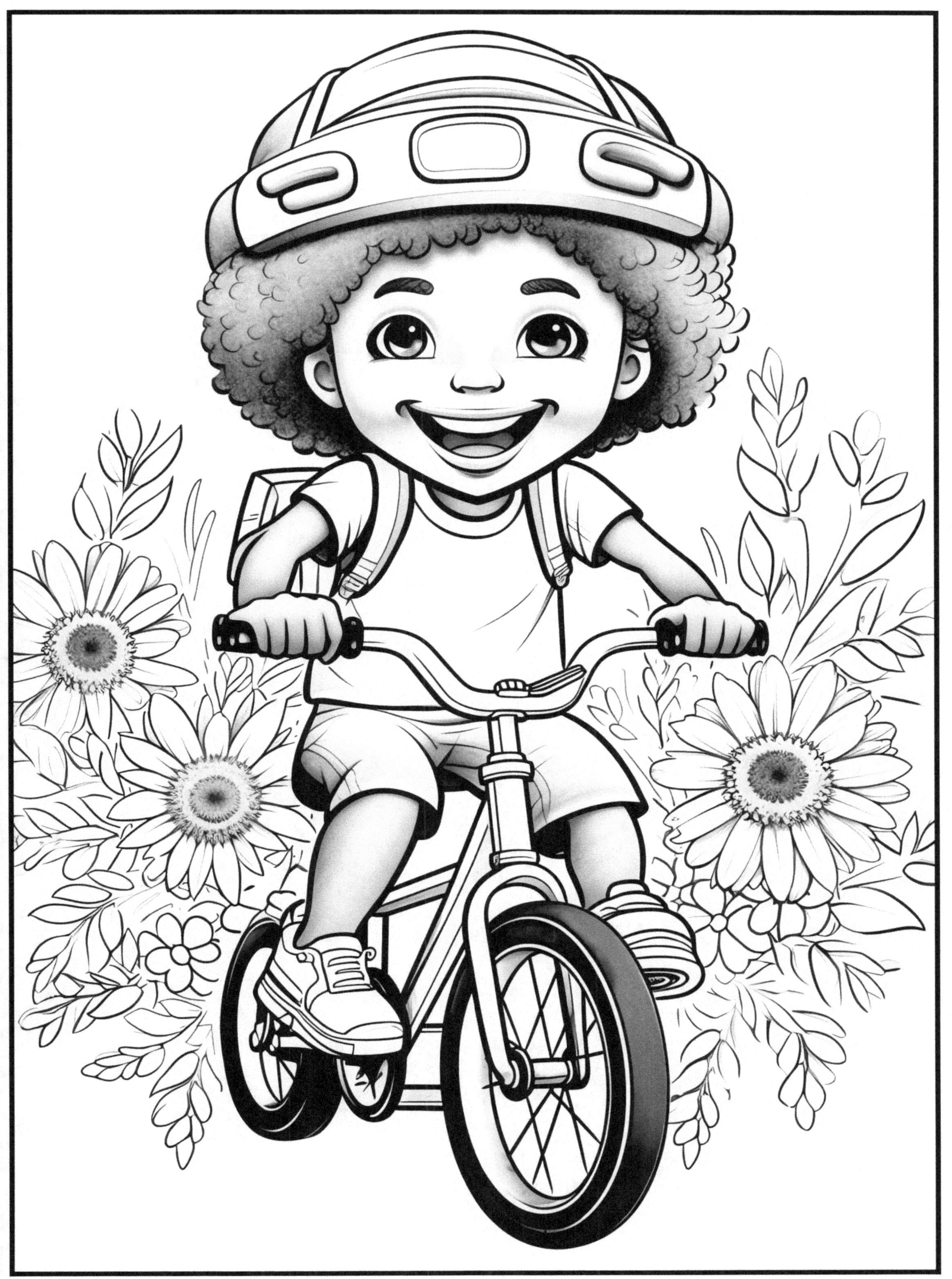

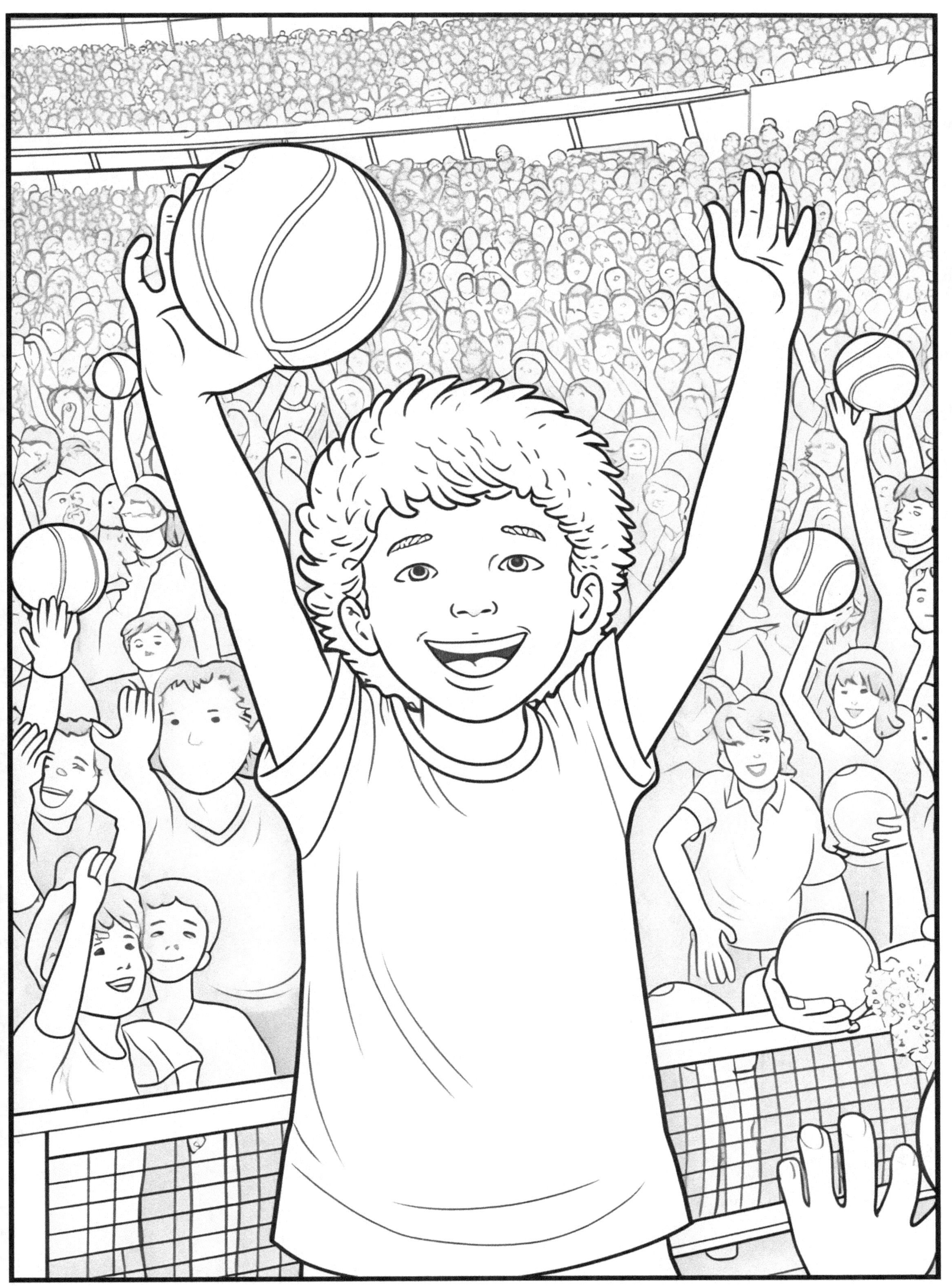

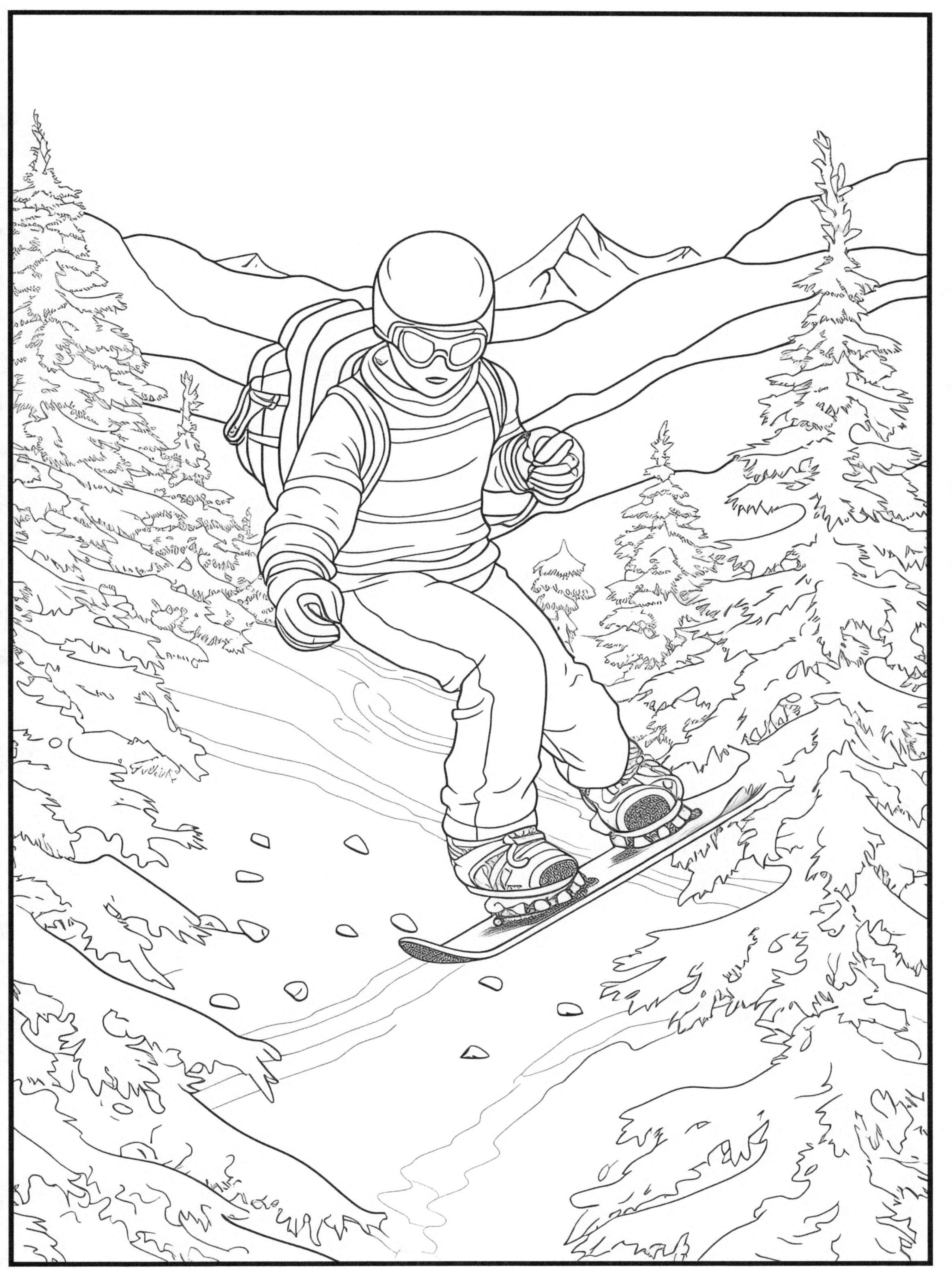

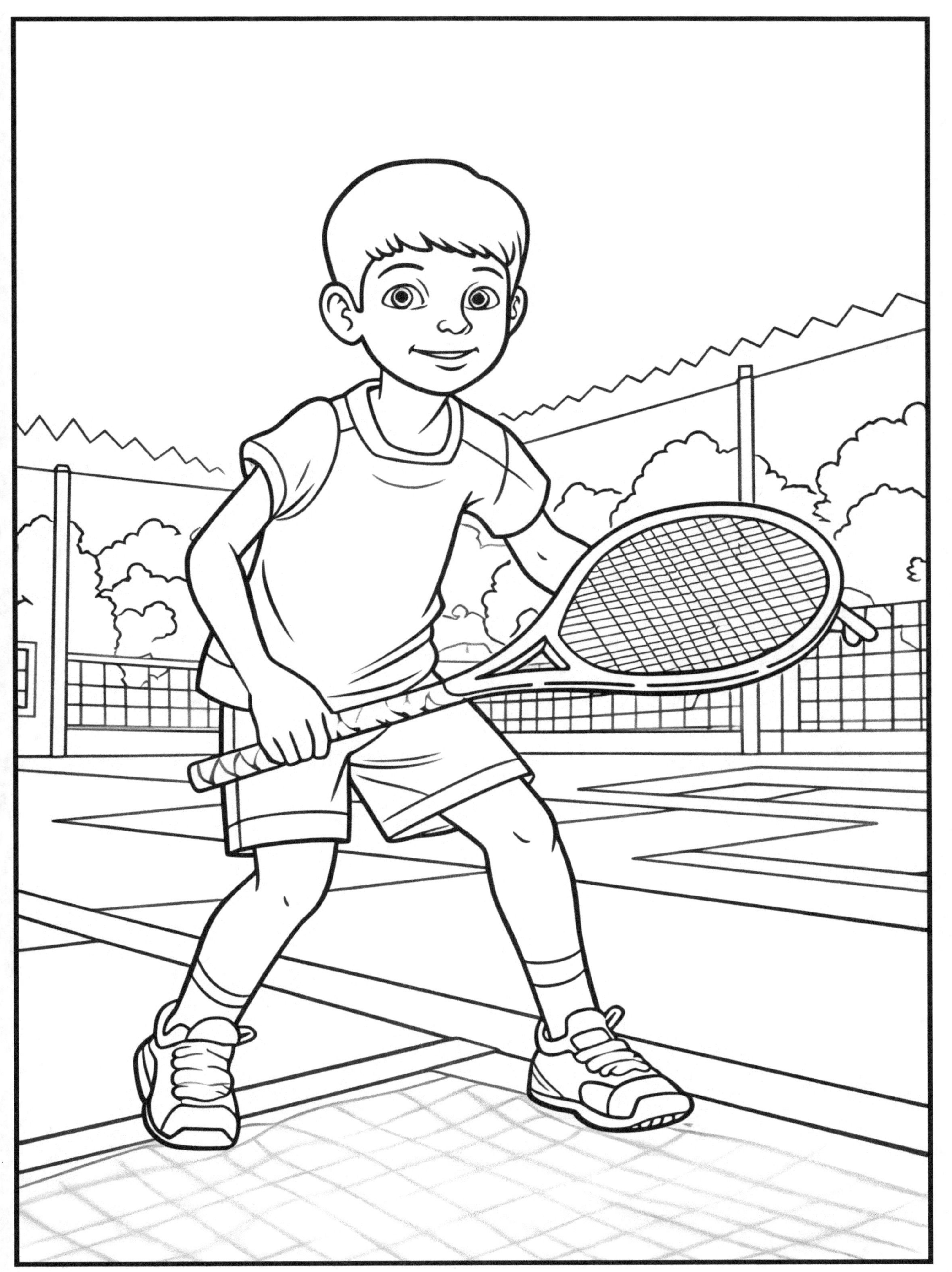

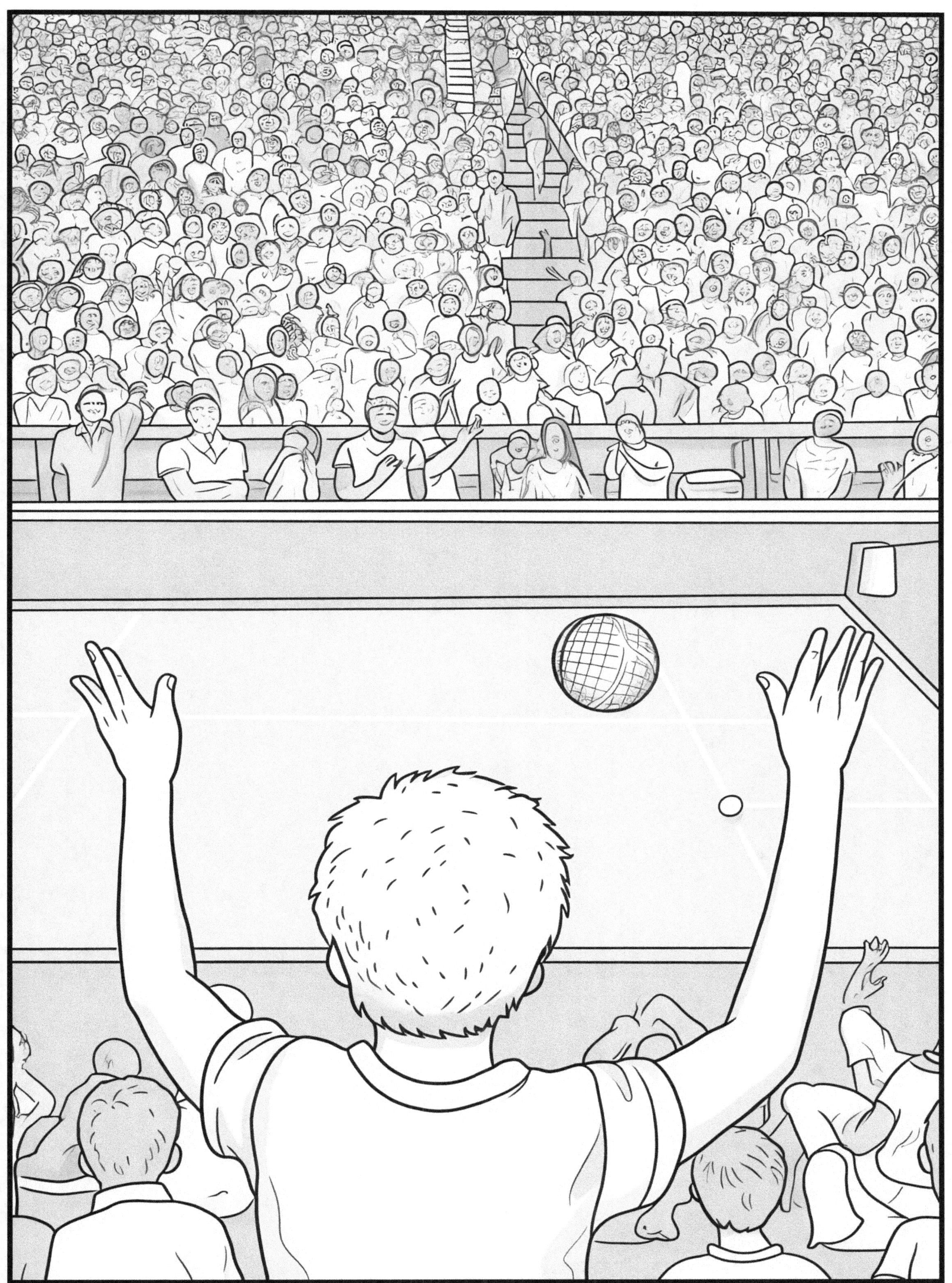

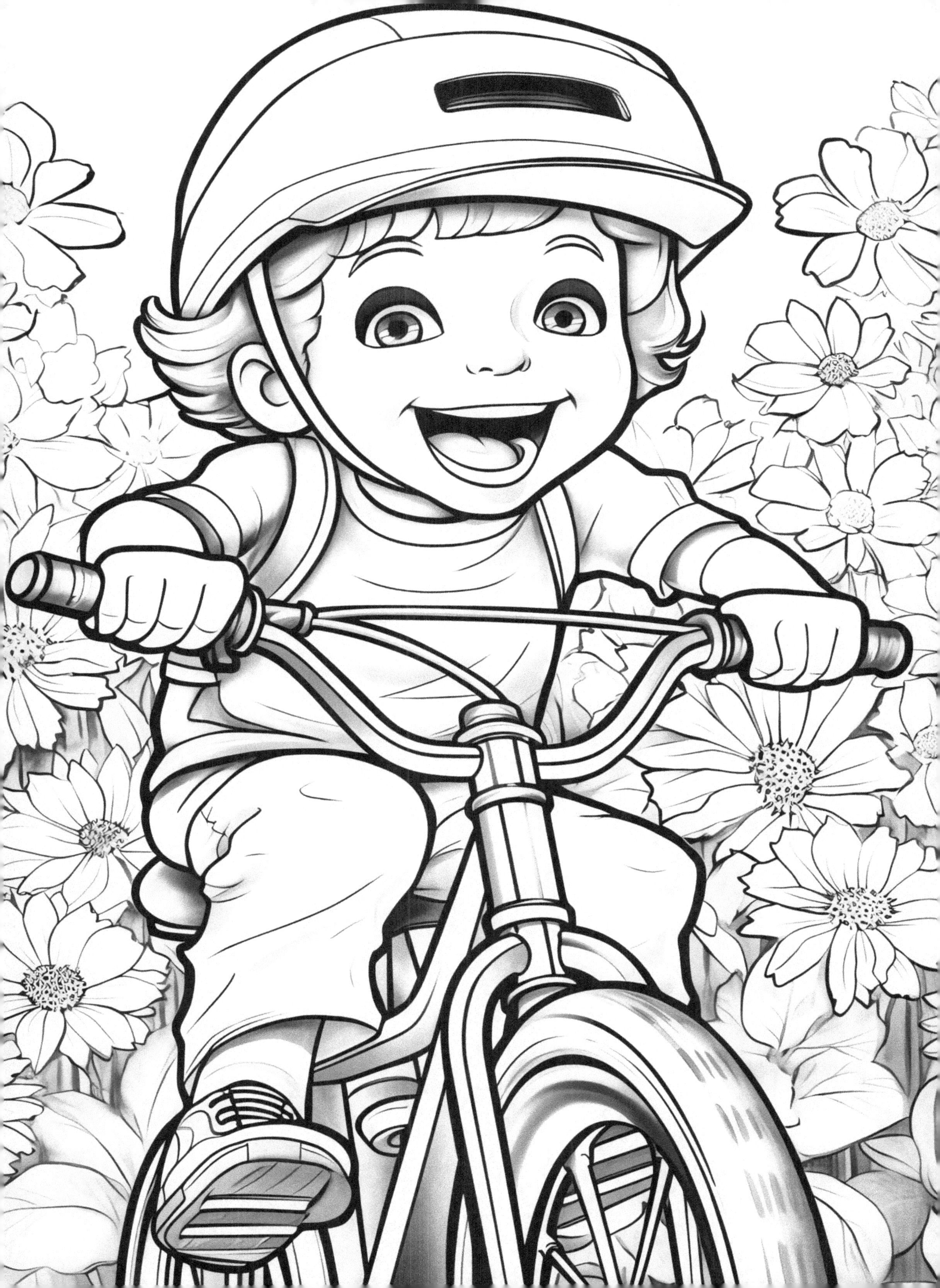

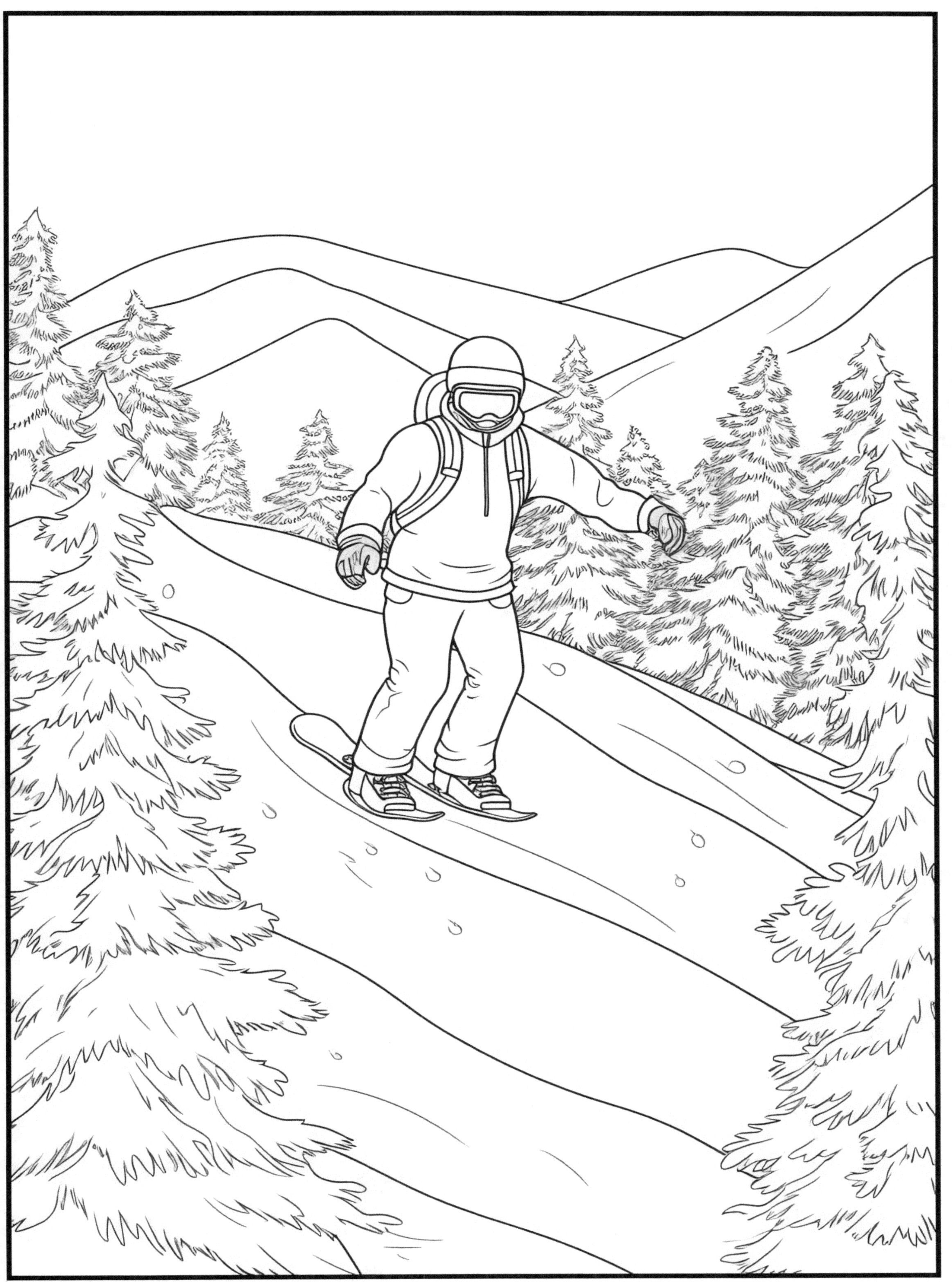

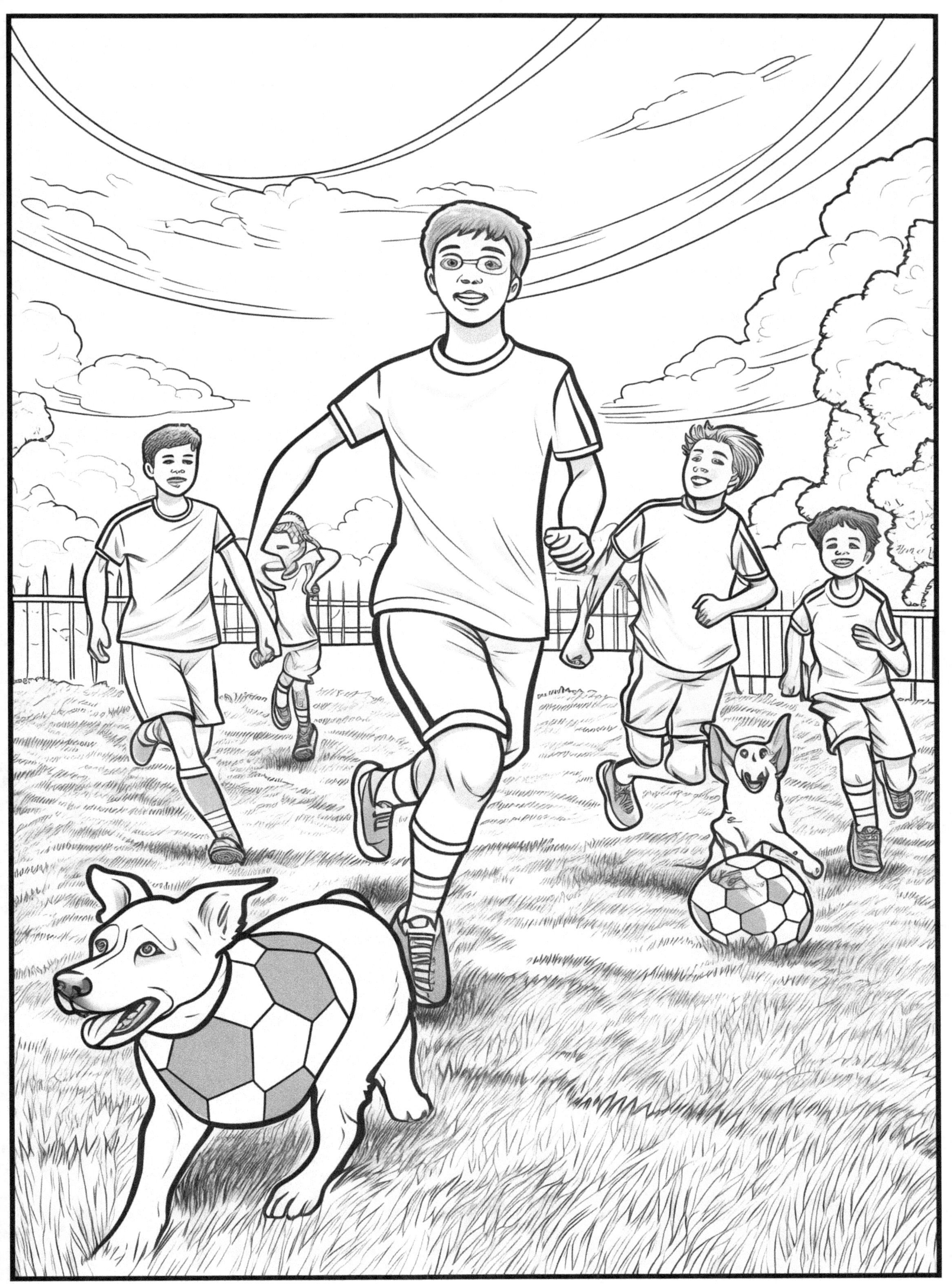

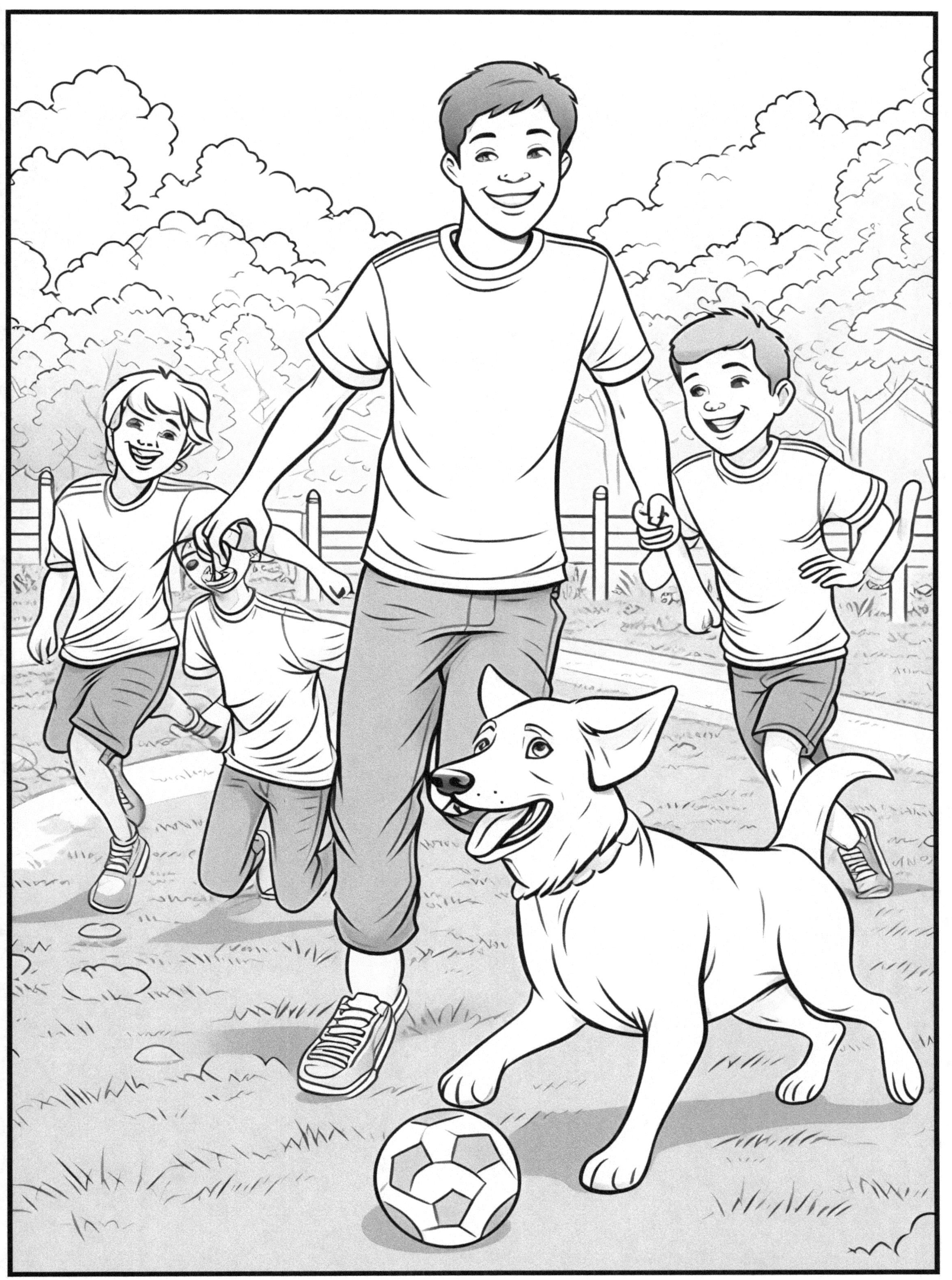

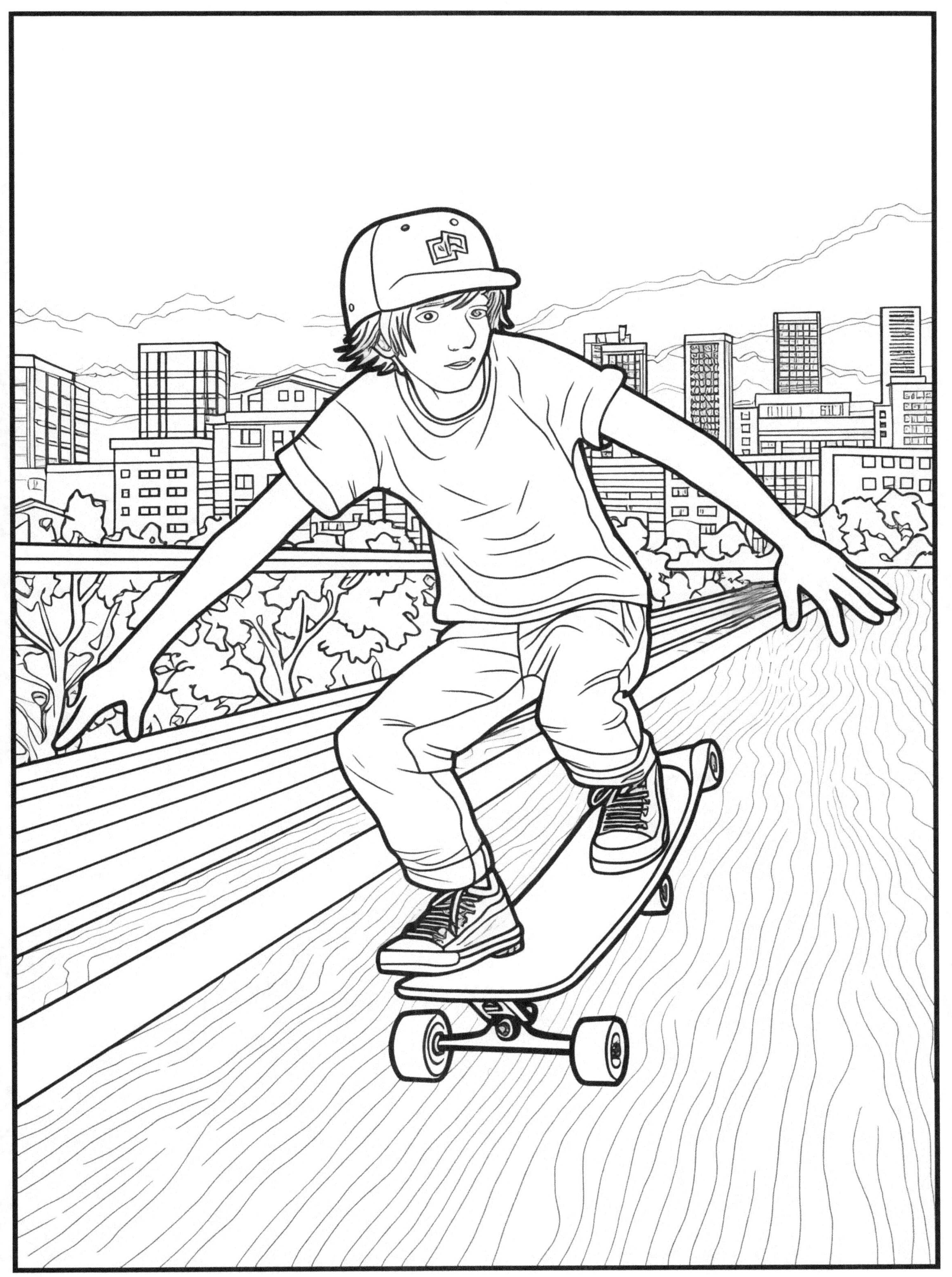

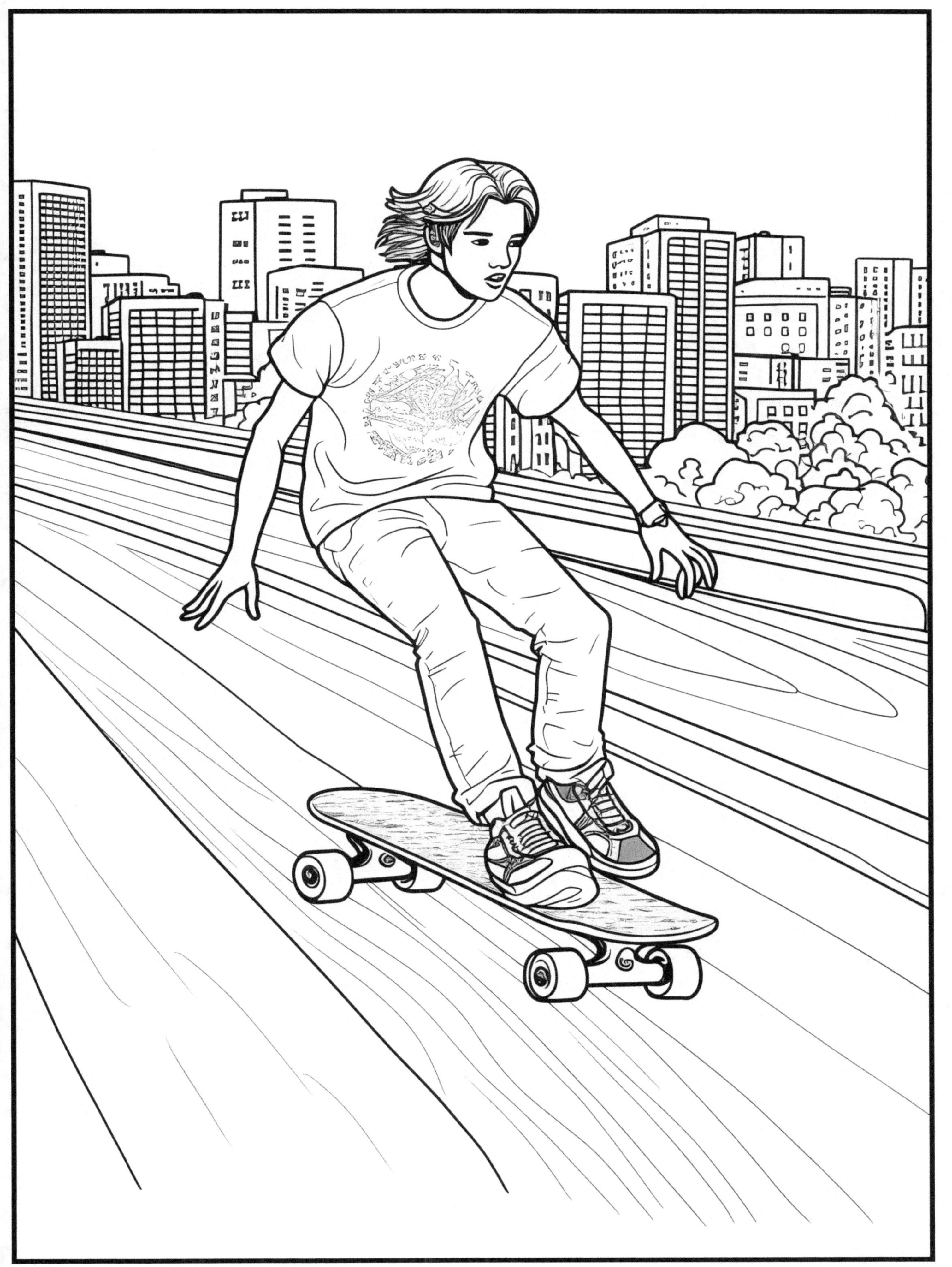

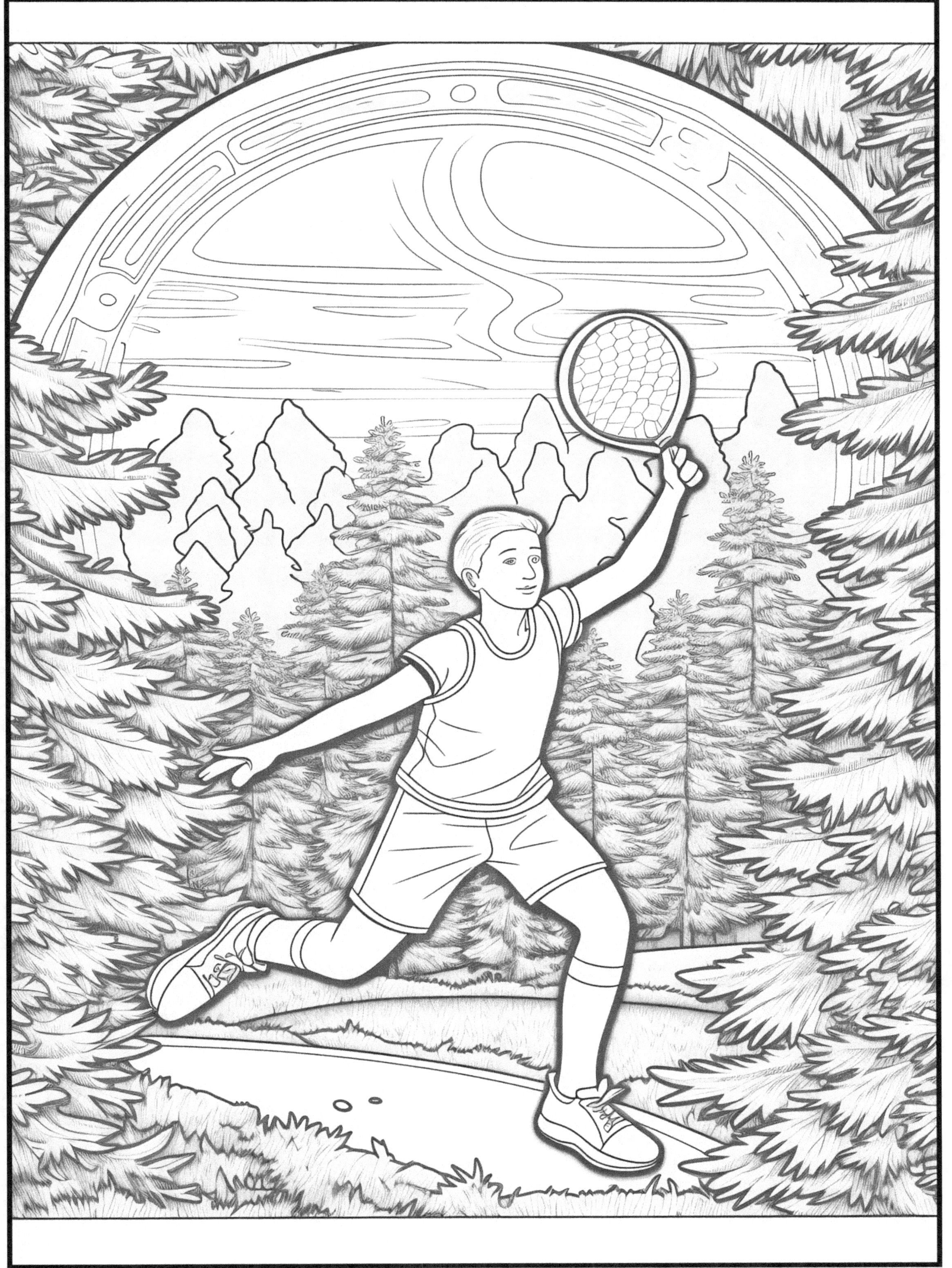

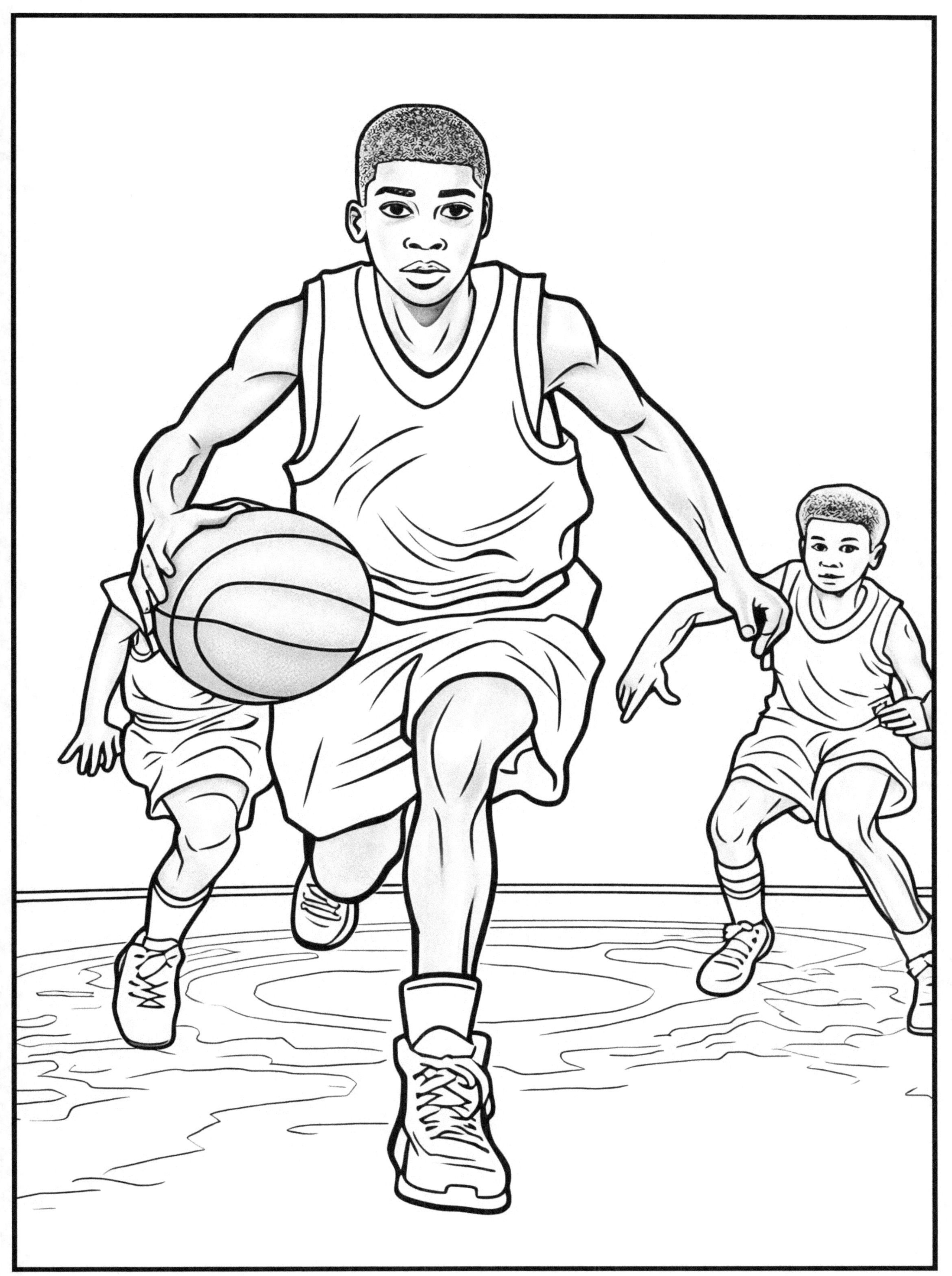

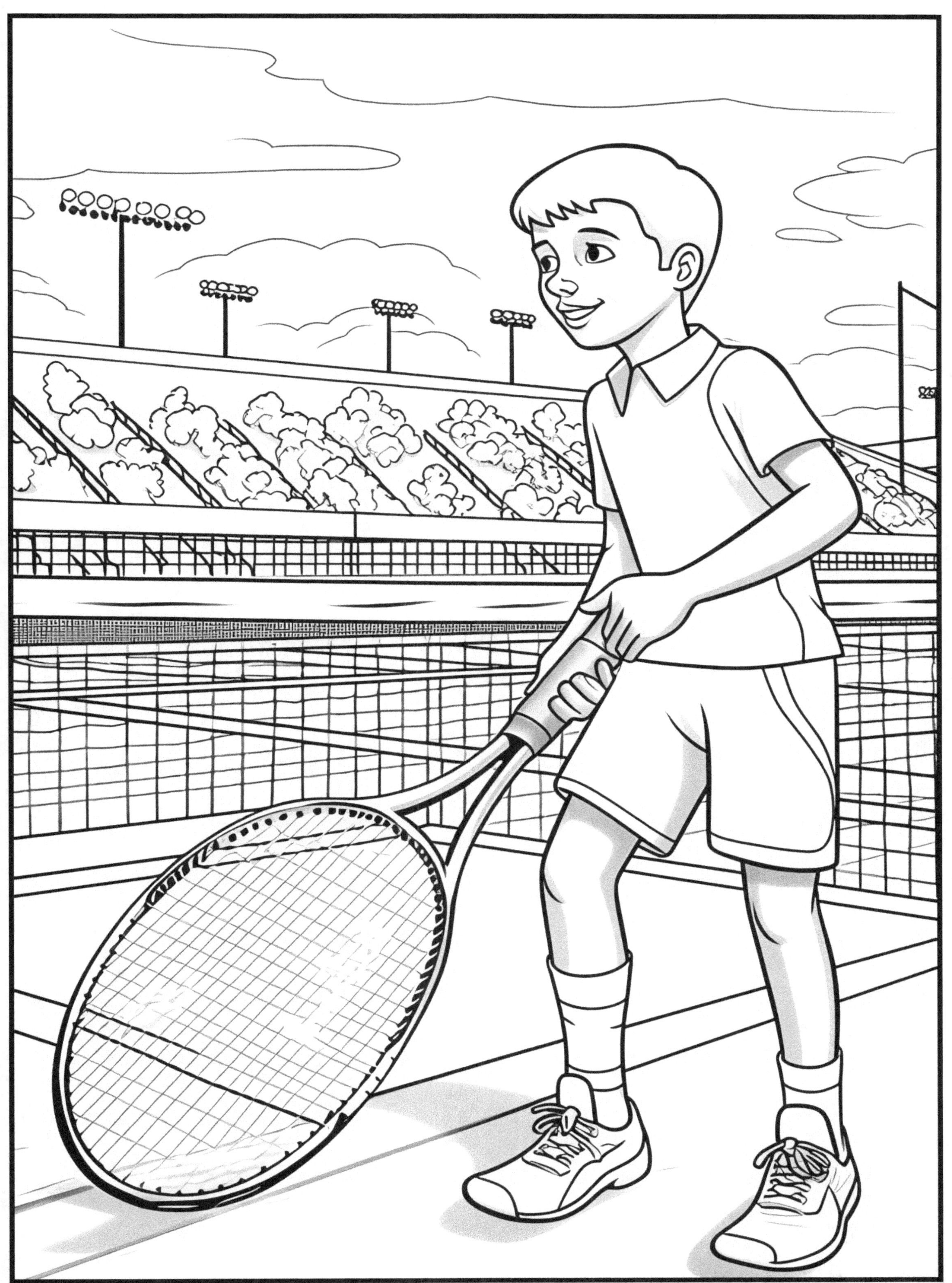